Charles
Associate Pro
Uni

D1187043

P rofessor Charles Mathewes is Associate Professor of Religious Studies at the University of Virginia, where he teaches religious ethics, theology, and philosophy of religion. He and his wife, Jennifer Geddes, are the coprincipals of Brown College at Monroe Hill, one of the University of Virginia's residential colleges.

Professor Mathewes lived in Saudi Arabia between the ages of 8 and 15. He received his B.A. in Theology from Georgetown University, graduating Phi Beta Kappa, and his M.A. and Ph.D. in Religion from the University of Chicago. He has lived in Charlottesville, Virginia, since 1997, making it the place he has lived longest by far.

Professor Mathewes is the author of *Evil and the Augustinian Tradition* and *A Theology of Public Life*, both from Cambridge University Press; *Understanding Religious Ethics*, from Wiley-Blackwell; and *The Republic of Grace: Augustinian Thoughts for Dark Times*, from Eerdmans. He served as editor of *The Journal of the American Academy of Religion*, the flagship journal in the field of religious studies, from 2006 to 2010 and was the journal's youngest editor ever. He is also associate editor of the forthcoming third edition of the *Westminster Dictionary of Christian Ethics* and serves on the House of Bishops Theology Committee of the Episcopal Church.

Professor Mathewes has received a number of teaching awards. Every year since 1999, his classes have been named as exemplary classes for prospective students to attend during the Days on the Lawn decision period for applicants accepted into the University of Virginia. In 2007, he received a Mead Honored Faculty award—one of the university's highest teaching awards—as well as a Mead Endowment Teaching Award to fund a dream idea. He used the endowment to run a small seminar on religion and politics that culminated in a trip to Washington DC and a meeting with politicians, policy experts, and legal scholars.

When Professor Mathewes and his wife are not residing in Brown College, they live with their children outside Charlottesville, in the foothills of the Blue Ridge Mountains. ■

Why Evil Exists

Charles Mathewes, Ph.D.

THE
GREAT
COURSES®

PUBLISHED BY:

THE GREAT COURSES
Corporate Headquarters
4840 Westfields Boulevard, Suite 500
Chantilly, Virginia 20151-2299
Phone: 1-800-832-2412
Fax: 703-378-3819
www.thegreatcourses.com

Table of Contents

Table of Contents

Table of Contents

Table of Contents

Why Evil Exists

Scope:

“It is not God I do not accept,” Dostoevsky grumbled, “but the world he has created.” In fact, the earliest literatures grapple with a question as troubling now as it was 4,000 years ago: Why do evil and suffering exist in the world?

From the ancient Sumerian *Epic of Gilgamesh* to the terror attacks of 9/11, the problem of theodicy—explaining the existence of evil in a divinely governed or morally ordered world—has been at the heart of every major religion and many secular philosophical worldviews, as well. Charting the various formulations of this problem and the different answers people in the West have given to it are the goals of this course. These lectures examine the history of cultural definitions of the problem of evil and the “solutions” devised for living in its shadow.

The problem of evil encompasses both “natural” and “moral” evil. Certainly, human suffering due to nature—death, disease, natural disasters, and the like—is troubling enough. But human malice adds an entirely distinct kind of difficulty, for human evil comes out of humanity’s distinctively moral character. The same energies of intellect and will that led mankind to cure innumerable diseases and put men on the moon led us also to poison gas and ICBMs; the capacities for emotional attachment and imaginative empathy that led to the expansion of fellow-feeling and genuine compassion for others we will never meet have led equally to our fear and hatred of those same others at other times. We will never lack for the ironic evidences of humanity’s conflicted and unstable condition—the strange and, at times, terrible alloy of nobility and brutality that together define our character. What does the fact of human cruelty and malice tell us about the ultimate fate of morality and religious belief? How best should we understand such malice, and how might we best respond to its reality in our lives and the lives of those around us?

These are some of the challenges the study of evil must confront. But things are more complicated still. In fact, the questions clustered under the title "the problem of evil" are not easily reduced to a single clear and precise problem; rather, the problem is itself a problem, a "meta-problem," so to speak, a problem whose proper form is itself up for debate and dispute. When we speak of evil, are we referring to a natural force of some sort, welling up from the most primitive part of our brain? Or does evil refer to a series of willed or learned capacities into which we are trained by our elders? Or is it something else entirely?

Answers to these questions inform the response a thinker or a culture gives to the problem, because they give determinate form to the problem itself. That is to say, a particular interpretation of the problem of evil is naturally shaped by one's sense of the precise scope of the problem, and one's proposed response to evil is also in large part determined by what one thinks evil is.

Here, then, are some of the questions thinkers have asked and, thus, questions that we must ask, as well:

1. Is evil something real or merely the result of human (psychological?) confusions?

2. Is evil its own power, or is it totally parasitic on other realities, and if so, which realities?

3. Is evil naturally part of the world or (perhaps more precisely) of our innate motivations and desires, or is it something we create by our own action?

4. How is evil related to our individuality? Must we be wicked to be unique individuals?

5. Is evil inescapable for humans? How best can we resist or contain evil?

6. Can we understand evil? That is, is there a way to make evil actions totally intelligible to us? Should we want such intelligibility at all?

7. Ought we to go on using the language of "evil" at all? Or is it so connected with our troubles that we need some entirely new language with which to understand our world?

In this course, we will examine the history of cultural definitions of the problem of evil, and we will explore a wide range of proposals that have been devised for living in its shadow. Texts and writers under discussion include the ancient Sumerian Epic of Gilgamesh, the Hebrew Bible, Greek tragedies, the Christian New Testament, the Qur'an, and Jewish Rabbinic thought; traditional authorities, such as Aristotle, Augustine, Aquinas, and Plato; major writers, such as Dante and Milton; modern thinkers, including Hume, Leibniz, Voltaire, and Nietzsche; and subsequent commentators, such as Martin Buber, Reinhold Niebuhr, Hannah Arendt, Albert Camus, and Joseph Conrad. Lectures focus on historical, philosophical, and religious perspectives in tracing the history of an age-old and extremely vexing problem: our basic investigation into the inner history of evil in the world and the implications of that history for the future. In undertaking this inquiry, we hope both to gain a deeper purchase on evil's manifestations, character, and effects and to understand the challenges evil presents to life in our world. ∎

The Nature and Origins of Evil
Lecture 1

> [I]s it possible for a theory to accommodate the enormously different empirical realities that we name with the term "evil"? Can any theory account for how to connect up genocides of international scale on one side and parents who beat their children on the other; can any theory account for all that? Hard to know.

The 20ᵗʰ-century Polish poet Zbigniew Herbert wrote that history is a "strange teacher." It teaches us by indirection, surprise, and pain, conveying lessons that are "dense and dark," difficult to understand. Our task in this course will be to grapple with those lessons in an effort to shed light on some of the most profound questions of human history, most fundamentally, the problem of evil.

This lecture series looks at how humans, especially in the West over the past five millennia, have thought about the origins and nature of evil. Why does evil exist, and what exactly is evil? Is it a function of humans living together in society, or is it somehow superhuman? Is evil an inevitable part of the cosmos, or is it something that we created and, thus, can possibly constrain or eliminate?

Let's start by defining evil: It's something that is not just against the moral order but intentionally and willfully against that order. Evil embodies a dimension of rebellion, although this rebellion needn't be directly experienced as such by those engaged in it. People can do evil without thinking too much about the acts they are performing. In fact, people who perform evil acts—genocide, abuse of racial or ethnic minorities—often understand themselves to be obeying the moral order of their particular culture. Part of the power of evil is the way it insinuates itself intimately into people's lives.

We can identify three broad families of theories about evil. The first of these locates evil in a kind of folly, a wholly irrational eruption of chaos in an ordered world. In this tradition, some thinkers have talked about evil as privational, as depriving creation of goodness and being, depriving reality itself of some dimension or thickness or depth. This is ultimately an optimistic vision, though it also suggests a certain disturbing capacity on the part of creatures to revolt against the moral order they inhabit. This account gives us an illuminating psychological picture of humanity, but at the same time, it may be too abstract. It's not clear how the idea of evil as the absence of being could help someone when confronting evil. Further, this view doesn't seem to account for the positive power of evil, the terrible sincerity it sometimes encompasses.

Part of the power of evil is the way it insinuates itself intimately into people's lives.

A second view sees evil as fundamentally part of the cosmos, part of our natural makeup. This naturalist view helps to domesticate evil by rendering it part of our character. Evil does not appear with any satanic magnificence or any kind of alienated theological aroma; it's a part of our world. But the grim thought that evil is all too human can become the source of hope. We may not be able to defeat evil entirely—because its home is our world—but at least we are struggling with a force that is nothing other than ourselves. The difficulty with this view is that the hope it offers may ultimately seem inadequate. What is the hope a hope for—to hold off evil only for the moment?

The third account we might characterize as "evil as maturation." Here, we see the idea that to become fully adult, it may be necessary to undergo some painful separation from our too-familiar and cozy surroundings. Just as teenagers rebel against their parents to gain a sense of identity, so our moral maturation requires a rebellion against God or the moral order, a kind of wounding in order to gain wisdom. This view captures a certain dimension of evil's reality: It's true that some evil is a matter of lashing out at the world in misconstrued anger, but is it true that the purpose of all evil is our edification?

Of course, we're not only interested in theoretical insights but also with the practical advice recommended to deal with the challenge of evil in the way that challenge is construed. Whether we can test evil by direct confrontation, by trying to absorb it into ourselves as marks of our glorious martyrdom for God, by developing nonviolent practices to resist its assaults on us—these and many other practical proposals are all intimately related to particular theoretical visions of evil.

In these lectures, we'll explore humanity's thinking about evil from the ancient Near East through the 20th century. Along the way, we'll consider numerous underlying questions: Can any theoretical representation of evil capture its full reality? What is the relationship between evil and the gods or God, the absolute moral order? Is evil a matter of barbarism versus civilization, or is civilization itself complicit in evil? Most fundamentally, is any of this theoretical activity helpful in our attempts to inhabit a world filled with evil? ■

Suggested Reading

Adams and Adams, eds., *The Problem of Evil*.

Anderson, *Sin: A History*.

Bouchard, *Tragic Method and Tragic Theology*.

Bowker, *Problems of Suffering in Religions of the World*.

Larrimore, *The Problem of Evil: A Reader*.

Midgley, *Wickedness: A Philosophical Essay*.

Ricoeur, *The Symbolism of Evil*.

Russell, *The Prince of Darkness: Radical Evil and the Power of Good in History*.

Questions to Consider

1. Recall the three broad historical options presented for thinking about evil (evil as folly, evil as natural, evil as maturation). Initially, which of these options do you find most convincing and why?

2. What do you make of Herbert's assertion that *historia* is *magistra vitae* ("the teacher of life") and has provided us with "dark and dense material"? What can history teach us, and what are its limits?

Enuma Elish—Evil as Cosmic Battle
Lecture 2

In calling these stories—the myth of the *Enuma Elish* and the *Epic of Gilgamesh*—"myths," I'm not trying to be dismissive. When I say "myth," I mean the deep structures of the cultural unconscious, the foundational narratives and the frames by which people think in these cultures.

In this lecture, we look at two of the oldest sources of human thinking about evil: the creation myth of Babylon known as the *Enuma Elish* and one of the earliest stories about a human attempting to make meaning out of death and suffering, the *Epic of Gilgamesh*. These narratives express one of the most fundamental convictions humans have had about evil: the idea that evil has a cosmic and perhaps metaphysical reality beyond human beings.

The categories of good and evil are present from the earliest civilizations of the ancient Near East. Also central to the ancient Near Eastern world is what scholars call the "combat myth," in which the cosmos is a battlefield between good and bad divine powers. This combat myth gives rise to these cultures' cosmogonies (stories of how the world and the cosmos came to be) and theogonies (stories of the creation of the gods). The creation of humanity is usually the final act in the drama that begins with the origins of these gods. In these stories, the chaos gods are confronted, defeated, and destroyed by other, often younger hero gods.

The *Enuma Elish*, the Babylonian cosmogony myth, is the oldest combat myth we have. In the story, reality begins with two primeval gods, Apsu and Tiamat; they create other gods, all of whom live in Tiamat's body because there is nothing outside the gods. Conflict arises between the original gods and the later generations they created. Ultimately, Marduk, the grandson of Tiamat, kills his grandmother and forms the earth from her corpse. By these acts, he becomes the primary god in the Babylonian pantheon.

Several aspects of this myth are key to our thinking about evil. First, the chaos god Tiamat is not represented as the source of evil per se, though she is, in fact, prior to people and, perhaps, more profoundly part of the universe than hero/ordering gods, such as Marduk. The "evil" emotions—envy, hate, fear, murderousness—mark the victorious younger gods, including Marduk, as much as they mark the older gods. Evil, then, is in some way intrinsic to reality, but it is also in inevitable conflict with the forces of order. Because the cosmos is created in a struggle and out of the old cosmos, it may bear traces or be the ongoing site of this conflict between good and evil. This explains the persistence of evil: It is literally worked into the fabric of the cosmos.

Compare this account to that of creation in the book of **Genesis**, especially Genesis 1: "In the beginning, God created the heavens and the earth." Here, there is no struggle; "the deep" (*tehom*) over which God moves at the beginning of creation is passive before God's will. God sees what God has created and deems it good.

> **Because the cosmos is created in a struggle and out of the old cosmos, it may bear traces or be the ongoing site of this conflict between good and evil. This explains the persistence of evil: It is literally worked into the fabric of the cosmos.**

Although there are important differences between the Jewish and Christian understandings of Genesis, both traditions clearly see that the impetus of this text, unlike the *Enuma Elish*, is toward a world in which one God uniformly and without resistance creates the cosmos out of passive matter.

The *Enuma Elish* explains the cosmic order, but the question remains: What's the place of humans in this order? The gods look like humans, and humans are made from the blood of a god, but one thing distinguishes the two: Humans are mortal, and the gods are not. This question motivates the *Epic of Gilgamesh*, the first recorded attempt to understand and inhabit a world in which suffering occurs and perhaps a world in which suffering is partially constitutive of what makes us human.

In the *Epic*, the king of Uruk, Gilgamesh, is plunged into grief by the death of his close companion, Enkidu. To assuage his grief, Gilgamesh undertakes a quest to find the key to immortality but is told: "The life that you are seeking you will never find. When the gods created man they allotted to him death, but life they retained in their own keeping." Gilgamesh returns to Uruk, where the sight of the city walls prompts him to praise the enduring work of human hands. Perhaps this recognition of the achievement of human effort is a sign that Gilgamesh has begun, at the end of the epic, to find a way out of utter despair: a slow turning back toward a merely human life. A parallel work or perhaps a coda to the *Epic* recounts the moment of Gilgamesh's death but suggests that it is precisely the finitude of human life that is the basis of whatever joys we can have. As we journey through life in the same way as Gilgamesh, there comes a moment when we know that death is our future, and we must decide how to live in light of that knowledge. ■

Important Terms

Enuma Elish: Babylonian creation myth, in which the god Marduk establishes himself as king over the gods by defeating Tiamat, the chaos monster.

Genesis: First book of the Jewish and Christian Scriptures, which tells the story of God's creation of the world, the origin of evil, and the development of the people Israel.

Gilgamesh: Important surviving work from Mesopotamia in the 3rd millennium B.C.E., in which the hero, Gilgamesh, suffers as he searches for immortality and founds a city.

Suggested Reading

Dalley, *Myths from Mesopotamia: Creation, the Flood, Gilgamesh, and Others*.

Damrosch, *The Buried Book: The Loss and Rediscovery of the Great Epic of Gilgamesh*.

Forsyth, *The Old Enemy: Satan and the Combat Myth*.

Lecture 2: *Enuma Elish*—Evil as Cosmic Battle

Foster, *The Epic of Gilgamesh*.

Kramer, *The Sumerians: Their History, Culture, and Character*.

Mason, *Gilgamesh: A Verse Translation*.

Questions to Consider

1. The lecture suggests that "myths" need not be seen as untruths; rather, they are foundational stories that reflect the deep cultural assumptions of a civilization. In addition to the myths mentioned in the lecture, what other modern myths reflect important aspects of our culture? Do we have modern myths about evil—if so, what are they?

2. Based on the lecture's description of ancient Near Eastern culture—and the *Enuma Elish* specifically—how do you see these cultures in relation to our own? Do their beliefs about evil seem alien, or familiar, or both?

Greece–Tragedy and *The Peloponnesian War*
Lecture 3

> Here, [as] in the ancient Near East, there are many gods, but the gods are more like characters in a long-running drama series, like *Dallas* or *Dynasty*. ... [They] exist, in a weird way, beyond good and evil, indulging in cruelty as easily as they take affront at it, and in neither case does it seem that their judgment or actions are beholden to any ultimately moral framework.

We turn now to Greece, where what we might call "anarchic polytheism" emerged, that is, a belief in many gods without a single organizing moral order among them. This worldview resulted in at least two approaches to the problem of evil: among the Greek tragedians, such as Sophocles and Aeschylus, the idea that sometimes, out of sheer tragic providence, the fates decree that a human must be brought down, and for Thucydides, the even more disturbing idea that evil is due, simply and terrifyingly, to luck or chance.

For the Greeks, tragic drama was a crucial structure for reflecting on evil, fate, and luck in human affairs. In *Oedipus Rex*, the king of Thebes discovers that he has unknowingly killed his father, Laius, and married his mother, Jocasta. When the truth emerges, Jocasta commits suicide, and Oedipus blinds himself and begs for exile from Thebes. The play ends ambiguously, with the chorus chanting the famous

Dover Publications.

The role of fate, chance, and luck in *Oedipus Rex* speak powerfully of the terrible paradoxes of fate and responsibility that Greek tragedy was so good at communicating.

maxim ascribed to the Greek legislator Solon: that no one should be called happy until they are dead.

The range of meanings and the role of chance in this play speak powerfully of the terrible paradoxes of fate and responsibility communicated by so much of Greek tragedy. One of the most traumatic elements of the play is that Oedipus is the vehicle for his own self-destruction; he recognizes this responsibility but also sees an unpredictable fate as guiding events. He thinks of himself as someone who has been humbled by the gods for an arrogance he did not quite see.

Sometimes, these plays seem to locate responsibility more directly in the gods themselves, to the point where humans become angry at the gods for their misfortunes. At the end of Sophocles's play *The Women of Trachis*, Hyllus attributes to the gods the cruel fate that has befallen his father, Heracles. He says, "Let the gods, their ruthlessness, their cruelty, be remembered./They take us to be their children, and call themselves Father,/and yet they well see such suffering." The moment is equivalent to a Christian or a Jew declaring the Holocaust to be, in some sense, the accomplishment of God's will.

The idea that fate has many strange twists, can turn strength against the strong, and can bring the mighty down became very pointed in the experience of the Peloponnesian War, captured in Thucydides's book on that conflict. The war was fought between Athens and Sparta, with allies on both sides, from 431 to 404 B.C. It was a devastating conflict, enabling the spread of plagues, starvation, and the ruin of the economies of the Greek world.

Thucydides's account of the war is largely an attempt to see in history a tragedy. He writes "against" the earlier historian Herodotus, who saw history and culture as natural forces that shaped character in certain ways. Thucydides, in contrast, saw people's decisions not as determined by their natural environment or cultural presuppositions but shaped by the political pressures of the moment. He believed not in determinism but in the accidental nature of things.

When he talks about the idea of motivations, Thucydides identifies an important theme that remains pertinent for us today, namely, that the human psyche in war is slowly deformed by the pressure of constant fear. Indeed, the war itself was caused by the Spartans' fear for their independence in the face of Athens's increasing hegemony over the Greek world. Once the war is started, it takes on a life of its own and begins to master the combatants. Each side hopes to exhaust the other before its own people and resources are exhausted. And neither considers the moral costs of the war—the damage and deformation it will do to their souls.

> **When he talks about the idea of motivations, Thucydides identifies an important theme that remains pertinent for us today, namely, that the human psyche in war is slowly deformed by the pressure of constant fear.**

At one point in the war, the Athenians sought the support of the small, insignificant island city of Melos against the Spartans. The Melians refused, and the Athenians responded by besieging Melos, eventually massacring the men and enslaving the women and children of the city. Afterward, the Athenians suffered a string of defeats and ultimately lost the war, yet Thucydides does not view their defeat as morally deserved because of their unnecessary cruelty to the Melians. Rather, it is, as the Athenians themselves had predicted, the wheel of fate turning; now cruelty will be done to them, not as payback but as part of the inevitable chaos and randomness of life.

For Thucydides and the Greek tragedians, there is no simple or straightforward moral order; all our moral actions are subject to dramatic reversal or deformation, and there are no guarantees that our moral sincerity will not, in fact, turn out to be destructive, perhaps even self-destructive. Further, Thucydides introduces into Western consciousness the idea of the accident, the possibility that evil and suffering may well have no cause at all. ■

Important Term

Oedipus Rex: Greek tragedy written by Sophocles, an Athenian tragedian.

Suggested Reading

Grene and Lattimore, trans. and eds., *The Complete Greek Tragedies*.

Padel, *In and Out of Mind: Greek Images of the Tragic Self.*

Thucydides, *The Landmark Thucydides*, Strassler, ed., Crawley, trans.

Thucydides, *The Peloponnesian War*, Lattimore, trans.

Williams, *Shame and Necessity*.

Questions to Consider

1. As we have seen, the Greeks added an important theme in Western thinking about evil by the introduction of the concept of tragedy. What do you see as the relationship between tragedy and evil? How are they connected, and how are they different?

2. Greek tragedians, such as Sophocles, as well as Thucydides offered varying answers to the causes of evil—is evil the result of destiny, or decision, or chance? What insights do you think these authors offer for understanding the causes of evil? What is the relationship between destiny and decision in creating evil?

Greek Philosophy—Human Evil and Malice
Lecture 4

The disagreements between [Plato and Aristotle] and their mutual opposition to tragedy echo down through the rest of the Western philosophical and religious traditions. The debates these guys had in a small corner of Greece 1,500–2,500 years ago have really, incredibly, shaped everything that came after that.

The Greek tragic tradition met a kind of internal resistance in the Greek philosophical tradition. The philosophers of Greece certainly took reality and history seriously, but they were also interested in assessing the strengths and weaknesses of people's views of reality in order to determine how best to think about evil and tragedy.

We begin with **Plato**, whose thinking about evil developed significantly over time. In his early dialogues, he seems to have thought that evil is a consequence of ignorance, that no one goes against a well-formed judgment, and that such judgment can never be truly evil. Evil here is a matter of "miseducation," which can be corrected by better information. Today, we, too, often believe that evil is simply a matter of ignorance that could be eliminated if people were properly educated.

As time went on, Plato's views darkened. By the middle of his life, he understood "evil" in a more profound and troubling way, and his depiction of the differences between good and bad people became far more radical. The character Thrasymachus in Plato's *Republic*, for example, represents a crucial problem for social order and harmony.

Plato (428–347 B.C.E.) was a disciple of Socrates and the teacher of Aristotle.

© Photos.com/Thinkstock.

Thrasymachus is a Sophist, a teacher of political rhetoric, and he argues with Socrates that justice is nothing more than the interest of the stronger. When he can't intimidate Socrates into agreeing with him, Thrasymachus withdraws into surly silence. Despite Plato's earlier idea that evil is, in some sense, ignorance, we can see that no amount of new information will help this character. He doesn't want to change or learn; he wants only to dominate. For Plato, goodness remains the properly intelligible thing to do, but unintelligibility—the irrationality of evil—has become more profound and radical in the human character.

Thrasymachus represents a terrifying challenge to Plato—and remember, it was people like Thrasymachus who would order Socrates to be killed. Plato confronts us with a frightening question: How should we live in a world that is often governed by people like Thrasymachus, those who are not on the way to becoming intelligible creatures? Can we bring the wholly irrational into the realm of reason, and if not, can we improve the social order so that the wholly irrational is not so prevalent in the future? Evil is not so easily captured here in descriptions of ignorance; it seems more tenaciously part of our world, more difficult to correct, and requiring far more fundamental changes for us to be unsusceptible to its attractions than the mere delivery of information to those caught in its clutches.

Plato also sees evil as a failure to be properly aligned with the moral order and, thus, with the good. Thrasymachus represents the person caught in a tyrannical soul—a disordered soul. And a tyrant, for Plato, tyrannizes himself before anyone else. He revolts against the conditions of his own creation. That's the mature picture of evil that Plato offers: one in which evil is a form of revolt against the conditions of our own creation and one that spreads evil through human society by infecting others with a misorientation to the good through erroneous cultural standards.

Aristotle, in contrast, explores the nature of evil in a far more "mundane" way through his discussion of *akrasia*, weakness of will. As Plato did, Aristotle thought that people could be wrongly habituated, but Aristotle saw neither good nor bad habits as rational. Humans are not simply aligned to the good, and evil is not a rupture of that relationship; humans are as much flesh as they are mind, and the flesh shapes a good deal of human behavior. For Aristotle, the goal is to find a happy medium in which the mind and the body interact responsibly, with distinct, harmonious interests and ends.

Evil here is not a radical rejection of intellect for flesh; it's more mundane than that. It's not an absolute revolt against nature but a misordering, a jumbling of our natural drives. Because Aristotle has a more moderate picture of humans than Plato, his picture of evil is also less dramatic. For Aristotle, humans exist on a continuum, which means that not all people can be made better. In this, he can be seen as offering a kind of "medicalizing" of evil, treating it as an unfortunate pathology. Nonetheless, both Aristotle and Plato are united in their skepticism about the possibility for radical human change after childhood.

Aristotle (384–322 B.C.E.) has a more moderate picture of what humans are, and therefore his picture of evil is less dramatic than Plato's.

As we'll see, the struggle between the Platonist and the Aristotelian views of the ultimate nature of evil—between evil as a kind of metaphysical revolt and evil as a mundane challenge—will echo across the rest of this lecture series. ∎

Names to Know

Aristotle (384–322 B.C.E.). Born in Stageira as a member of the aristocracy. Eventually, Aristotle made his way to Athens, became a disciple of Plato, and studied at Plato's Academy for almost 20 years.

Plato (428–347 B.C.E.). Born in Athens, the son of Ariston, a prominent aristocrat. As a young man, Plato seems to have traveled extensively before returning to Athens, with ambitions to be a poet; there, he became a disciple of Socrates.

Important Term

akrasia: An ancient Greek term that Aristotle uses for "weakness of will." Suggests an explanation for evil as a pathology of moral motivation, a divided, incoherent, or "weak" will.

Suggested Reading

Aristotle, *Nichomachean Ethics*, Irwin, trans.

Aristotle, *Poetics*, Janko, trans.

Nussbaum, *The Fragility of Goodness: Moral Luck in Greek Tragedy and Philosophy*.

Plato, *Gorgias, Menexenus, Protagoras*, Schofield, ed., Griffith, trans.

Plato, *The Republic*, Grube and Reeve, trans.

Questions to Consider

1. Plato and Aristotle had different views concerning the nature of evil and its relation to human life. How do you see Plato's and Aristotle's views reflected today? Do people tend to see evil as a radical challenge or a mundane one?

2. For the early Plato, evil was primarily a matter of ignorance rather than malice. What do you see as the relationship between evil and knowledge? Can we tell good and evil apart clearly? Can evil be combated through education, or is the problem more pervasive?

The Hebrew Bible—Human Rivalry with God
Lecture 5

> [O]ne of the ways we keep these texts at a safe distance from ourselves is by imagining that they were written down by people in a time of unimaginable strangeness compared to our own, unimaginably distant from ours. ... But if we believe that, we insulate ourselves from the possibility that these texts were written down by people like us and have something directly to say to us about our common human condition, and I think they do.

In this lecture, we turn to the Scriptures of the people Israel, in which we see a vision of evil as fundamentally a form of rebellion against a single, good, sovereign God. Further, the origins of evil are intertwined with a particular kind of human ambition that is first named here: the ambition to rival God.

The story of Adam and Eve follows a recounting of the creation that seems set against the combat myth paradigm of the ancient Near East. In Genesis, the world is wholly good, is seen as such, and is governed as such by a wholly good God. But for the ancient Israelites, we must note that the Fall did not represent the entry of evil into the world in a completely unanticipated way. Adam and Eve did not create evil out of nothing, as Christians believe God created the cosmos; rather, they are the first to actualize the potential for evil, which was part of the cosmic structure that God had created from the beginning. Despite the overall resistance of the text to the Babylonian combat myth, the Genesis account still suggests that evil and temptation were a potential presence in the world.

The language we get of Eve "seeing that the fruit was good to eat" suggests a perverted vision, a parody of God's seeing that the world is good. Eve's temptation is a temptation to behave as God does, the temptation to judge for herself, a temptation, that is, to theological sovereignty. As the serpent says, "You will be like God, knowing good and evil."

This raises a question: What exactly is the sin here? Is it the experience of temptation or the sheer disobedience of the will that prompts the act? And what

Adam and Eve do not create evil out of nothing. Rather, they are the first to actualize the potential for evil, which was part of the cosmic structure that God had created from the beginning. Theirs is only, as it were, the first failing, not the origin of all fault in the cosmos.

is it about the knowledge of good and evil that is so destructive for humans? The Hebrew root of the word "knowing" suggests an intimate experience more than a merely intellectual acquaintance. Such knowledge gives its knower a certain set of skills and a certain kind of maturity perhaps, but the Bible suggests that it is a flawed maturity. This knowledge is both accomplishment and burden, blessing and curse. The story seems to tell us that perhaps all such human maturity is accidental and reluctant; perhaps any real wisdom contains within itself a certain ambivalence about the cost incurred to gain that wisdom.

The nature of evil in Genesis is clearly a form of rebellion—a kind of rivalry against God—perhaps initially inadvertent, but then it compounds itself in Adam and Eve's flight and hiding from God. There seems to be a longing for rivalry with God, but at no point are humans actually able to rival God. Evil and rebellion have a fundamentally futile character in this story that the combat myth never contains. The fact that Adam also took the fruit suggests a strange community to evil. Once they have both eaten the fruit and their eyes are open, Adam and Eve work together. Evil is not simply an individual act; it is compounded and deepened by communality.

The story seems to tell us that perhaps all such human maturity is accidental and reluctant; perhaps any real wisdom contains within itself a certain ambivalence about the cost incurred to gain that wisdom.

With Adam and Eve's children, **Cain and Abel**, we see the pattern of rebellion continue, but this time, the rebellion has direct inter-human implications. Cain and Abel's story is about the dangers of resentment: Cain resents God's choice of Abel's sacrifice over his own and kills his brother. Such resentment warps our vision of what is important and comes to "master" us, just as God says sin will master us in the exchange with Cain about Abel's whereabouts. Cain's reply to God is an angry retort—"Am I my brother's keeper?"—suggesting that sin is now, outside of the garden, perpetually part of our lives, and we are engaged in a grim struggle against it.

Another biblical story, that of the Tower of **Babel**, exemplifies rebellion in an explicitly political way. Humans here are working in concert against God, to build "a tower whose top will reach into heaven." God's response is to render the world fractured among many different languages and people. A suspicion emerges here that carries forward even to today: the problematic unity of all mankind against God. Because it is so powerful, God fears the community of humans when it is separate from the right worship of God and from obedience to God.

In the Hebrew Bible, we see a relatively coherent picture of a God whose plans for humanity are straightforward and easy to manage, yet those plans are, in some completely inexplicable way, rejected by humans entirely. This tradition secures the goodness and sovereignty of God and the goodness and stability of the moral order as a whole, but at the cost of rendering the root motive for human evil thoroughly mysterious. ■

Important Terms

Babel: In the book of Genesis, the site where humanity attempts to construct a tower to heaven; often associated with Mesopotamian Babylon.

Cain and Abel: Sons of Adam and Eve in Genesis. The story recounts the murder of Abel by his brother, Cain, after God shows favor to Abel. Suggests that evil is now a permanent feature of human life that must be struggled against.

Suggested Reading

Anderson, *The Genesis of Perfection: Adam and Eve in Jewish and Christian Imagination*.

Levenson, *Creation and the Persistence of Evil*.

Questions to Consider

1. What is your response to this lecture's reading of the Genesis story? Is this a different telling of the Fall than you have heard before? Do you agree that the story suggests that Adam and Eve *actualize* (rather than create) evil in the world?

2. How do you see the Genesis account in comparison to others we have examined so far? Does the concept of rebellion against God presented throughout the Genesis stories add important dimension to the idea of evil? In what ways do you see the stories of Genesis continuing to exert influence on our conceptions of evil?

The Hebrew Bible—Wisdom and the Fear of God
Lecture 6

> Interestingly, the story of Job, the figure of Job, seems outside of the major narrative of the people Israel in the Hebrew Bible. … There's something important about Job here, something about the universality of his condition. He is not marked out as a member of the people Israel; he's simply a human.

One major strand of the Hebrew Bible sees evil as fundamentally a rebellion against God and God's good order. But another strand talks about evil and suffering in disquietingly different terms: as things perhaps willed directly by God. This strand raises questions about the nature of God's governance of human life, the mystery of God's dispensing of both good and evil to humanity, and humanity's proper response to a God who acts in such mysterious ways.

We begin with **Abraham** and the covenant. A covenant is not a contract because it is open-ended; it doesn't completely define the boundaries of the ethical relationship it creates. In many ways, a covenant is an act of faith and hope. Abraham's covenant with God gives him his life, but it is not a life without darkness.

When God tells Abraham that God is going to destroy

Dover Pictorial Archive Series.

The story of Sodom and Gomorrah is a story about judgment and justice.

24

Sodom and Gomorrah, Abraham begs God to spare the innocent, which God does. This crucial moment reveals that God and Abraham are not in a covenant of power but an ethical covenant. God makes known that God can be appealed to as a force for justice. But then God asks Abraham to kill his son. To sacrifice Isaac means effectively that Abraham must leave his family behind, just as God had asked him to leave his family in Chaldea and to leave behind his original name and identity. In many ways, the call to sacrifice Isaac is a call for Abraham to sacrifice himself.

The warning of Abraham's life—that God's ways are not our own—is made much more explicit still in the Book of Job.

This story tells us that God is far more foreign to our notions of right and wrong than we might at first realize. At times, God seems intent on destroying us, and we cannot complain because everything we are—our names, our identities, our children—is from God. Abraham's silence in the face of God's command seems somehow inhuman, as if there is something enormously profound in Abraham, but he knows he cannot communicate it. That is, he has some wisdom about life and God's expectations for us that we perceive in his silence precisely because he can't share it.

The warning of Abraham's life—that God's ways are not our own—is made much more explicit in the Book of Job. As we know, God allows Satan to inflict terrible suffering on Job, who then refuses the consolations of his friends and is ultimately told to curse God and die. In the end, God answers Job's complaints by telling him that he cannot know God's ways. Job's story seems to tell us that we shouldn't try to investigate evil, but it also raises important questions: If Satan is doing God's work, then is God allowing evil to happen or is God actively doing evil? And is there any real difference between the two?

Job's comforters give a voice to the readers of the Book of Job, both groups attempting to bring the apparent irrationality of Job's punishment into the realm of the intelligible. And Job's rhetorical duels with the comforters are the most important parts of the Book of Job because those duels establish his faithfulness. But does the story of Job's suffering offer us wisdom, or is it helpful only to those who have already suffered? One of the great puzzles of many of these texts is that it's not clear that the people who most need to hear the lessons they seek to convey are able to apprehend those lessons. It may be that we can't understand what such texts are trying to communicate until we have undergone similar experiences. If we think of Job as a "wisdom text," perhaps it is saying that real wisdom may be acquired only through intimate, first-person experience.

> **Job's comforters give a voice to the readers of the Book of Job, both groups attempting to bring the apparent irrationality of Job's punishment into the realm of the intelligible.**

The stories of Abraham and Job serve as puzzles and goads for the rest of the tradition in two distinct ways: First, they disturb the faithful's confidence that God's plans for humanity are wholly intelligible and entirely in agreement with our own wishes and aims. Second, they force us to question how a recognition of God's terrible mysteriousness might be achieved by us short of the trials put upon Abraham or the sufferings inflicted on Job.

The prophets of ancient Israel struggled with such questions. How can we be present in the world before God when we don't know how God will act toward us? As with Abraham and Job, the prophet Isaiah tells us that we can have no clear and certain knowledge; we can know only that the obedience called for will not necessarily be easy. A fearful reverence before God is probably the wisest course to take but also a course taken only by the wise. ∎

Abraham: Early patriarch of Israel whose story is recounted in Genesis. He makes a covenant with God and obediently follows God's command to sacrifice his son, Isaac, though God intervenes at the final moment.

Suggested Reading

Brueggeman, *The Prophetic Imagination.*

Heschel, *The Prophets.*

Kierkegaard, *Fear and Trembling*, Hong and Hong, eds. and trans.

Mitchell, *The Book of Job.*

Newsom, *The Book of Job: A Contest of Moral Imaginations.*

Scheindlin, *The Book of Job.*

Questions to Consider

1. The stories of Abraham, Job, and the Prophets presented a new development in thinking about evil—namely, the idea that evil may actually be an instrument of God's providence. What is your response to this? Can evil be a tool used by God to accomplish God's own purposes?

2. Is Abraham's obedience to God best seen as a contrast to Adam and Eve's rebellion? And should it disturb us that Abraham's obedience is proved by God commanding what seems to be an "evil" act?

> [S]omehow in the last century or so, lots of Christian churches have just simply ignored [the book of Revelation], like it's an unpleasant, smelly, aggressive relative who shows up to family gatherings but no one wants to talk to. This is a big mistake; this is a shame, because, in fact, the embarrassment of Christians to talk about this text ... makes them especially susceptible to ignoring a crucial dimension of the Christian message here.

Early Christian communities are often presented as small groups of gentle people living in the nooks and crannies of the Roman Empire, practicing their faith as far as possible from the centers of power. But far from being wholly pacifistic, early Christians saw themselves as bit players in a cosmic struggle between God and Christ, on the one hand, and the principalities and powers commanded by Satan, on the other. This "cosmic war" motif is visible in Paul's letters and comes to full fruition in the book of **Revelation**.

The early Christian tradition seemed to think that evil had declared war against God and the forces of goodness. Here, Christianity is developing the rebellion motif we saw in the Hebrew Bible, but it is now applied to angelic powers, as well as humans. The Gospel texts especially have a strong sense of the demonic powers as a vivid presence in the world. Recall that Jesus, at the beginning of his mission in the Gospel of Mark, is tempted by Satan in the desert, and many of his miracles are reported to have come at the expense of bad spirits. Indeed, a sense of a coming final battle with these evil spirits seems to lurk behind many stories in the Gospels. The fact that Jesus "set his face to go to Jerusalem" (Luke) tells us that a final confrontation with the satanic powers seems to have been inevitable to Jesus.

Later, Paul understood the churches to be caught in a struggle between God and Satan, with the outcome already decided, perhaps, by the Crucifixion and the Resurrection. Note here what Christian theologians refer to as the "already and not yet" motif. In Jesus's life, death, and Resurrection,

Christians believe that Satan has already been defeated and the world is already saved, though it has not yet come to its full salvation. The powers of evil are still afoot and can still fight back, and because of this, the faithful must equip themselves spiritually for a struggle.

In Revelation, the theme of a battle against supernatural powers is even more pronounced. An apocalyptic text, like the book of Revelation, speaks of the

© Dover Publications, Inc.

In the Gospels, Jesus seems alert to the presence of the demonic spirits, as in the Gospel of Mark, when Jesus is tempted by Satan in the desert.

end of the world and seeks to offer its readers a skeleton key to decipher the signs of the times. More basically, Revelation also aims to teach people how to live in this world in the end times. More than a collection of predictions about the end of the world, it is about the present world. The theme of combat again pervades this text, crystallized around the metaphor of combat between the "dragon"—an embodied force of evil—and a good God.

> **The powers of evil are still afoot and can still fight back, and because of this, the faithful must equip themselves spiritually for a struggle.**

Another dimension of the New Testament's heritage about evil is the idea of **original sin**. This doctrine seems to have gotten its start in the early Christian apprehension of the significance of the goodness of Jesus Christ. The earliest Christians clearly had a sense that the person—not the message—of Jesus Christ was, in some important way, theologically revelatory. For Jesus to be as good as Christians thought he was, the world must be pretty bad; for Jesus to be as powerful as they experienced Jesus as being, the enemies arrayed against him must be strong. Early Christians, thus, depicted the human condition more darkly and represented the powers of evil more dramatically than did others of their time. The sense of spiritual combat that already existed made evil more palpably and determinately part of creation itself.

The magnitude of God's activity that Christians perceived in Jesus's life, death, and Resurrection demanded a powerful opponent over whom to triumph, and that opponent had to be the force of evil insinuating its way into human history. Saint Paul, in his letters, looked back through the history of evil and found its beginnings in the story of Adam and Eve. For Paul, the story of Adam and Eve is not simply the first instance of a failure that had always been possible; it is the radical introduction of some new substance of malice and power that had not existed in the world before.

It's important to note that the notion of original sin doesn't mean that nature itself is evil; it's that we have appropriated our natures in a way that makes them evil. When God's kingdom comes to earth, Christ and everyone will be resurrected in the flesh. Salvation is not a matter of escaping the flesh but of properly inhabiting it. ■

Important Terms

original sin: Christian doctrine that stresses evil as dramatic, powerful, and endemic to the human condition.

Revelation: Apocalyptic text contained in the New Testament that describes the final cosmic battle between God and the forces of evil.

Suggested Reading

Kovacs and Rowland, *Revelation: The Apocalypse of Jesus Christ.*

Questions to Consider

1. Why do you think the concept of an apocalyptic cosmic struggle was so important to early Christian thought about evil? Is this concept still applicable or useful today?

2. In these New Testament texts, thinking about evil becomes amplified through Paul's understanding of original sin. Do you see Paul's reinterpretation of the Genesis story as a helpful Christian contribution or a deviation from the story's "true" meaning?

3. How is the contemporary Christian picture of the world similar to these early Christian texts? How is it different?

The Inevitability of Evil—Irenaeus
Lecture 8

> It would have been possible, for example, for someone not well versed
> in philosophy, not as able to speak philosophically and abstractly
> as Irenaeus was, to have first explained and given an account of
> Christianity, and in that case, the future of Christian thinking would
> have been very, very different.

C hristian theology has a tradition of offering what are known as
theodicies: theories of evil that make it intelligible and attempt to
explain how we can affirm the existence of a good, all-powerful God
in the face of the reality of evil. Two of these theodicies in particular have
been quite powerful: that of Augustine, which we will explore in the next
lecture, and that of Irenaeus.

Christian theology is relatively unique in comparison to other world religions
in its fixation on the problem of evil. Indeed, according to Christianity, the
world is far more profoundly mired in evil than our ordinary experience
suggests it might be. As we said in the last lecture, with the growing
recognition of the magnitude and power of Christ's saving work in the
world, the early Christian community was required to revisit its assessment
of worldly corruption, and in doing so, rethink and deepen its sense of the
sinfulness of the world.

Among the earliest thinkers who began to systematize the Christian account
of good and evil was **Irenaeus of Lyon**, generally considered to be the first
truly great church father. His greatest work is *Against Heresies*, written
in opposition to Gnosticism, a pseudo-philosophical movement popular
among elites in the ancient Mediterranean world. Gnosticism argued that
the materiality of the world is the source of evil and that humans in their
true essence contain a spark of innocence that must be unlocked from the
cage of flesh and allowed to escape. The Gnostics ultimately began to claim
Christianity as a form of Gnosticism, but for that to be true, Christianity had
to be understood as a radical renunciation of the Jewish story.

For someone like Irenaeus, Gnosticism threatened the Christians' vision of how they should live in the world, who their ancestors were, and who their rivals were in the present world. Irenaeus and the mainstream of orthodox theology in the Christian world argued that Christianity was a part of the story of the people Israel, although it offered a new version of that story. This view ensures that the Old Testament is read as an authentic story of God's dealing with humanity.

According to Irenaeus, humanity must succumb to sin, fall into sin, and receive its punishment, namely suffering and death. He offers the story of Jonah in the belly of the whale as an allegory for the human fall.

Irenaeus posits a picture of evil as an inevitable and necessary component of the development of the human race. He explains this by interpreting the story of Jonah in the belly of the whale as an allegory for the human Fall. Just as Jonah had to be swallowed by the whale, so must humanity succumb to sin and receive its punishment, namely, suffering and death. Then, God will raise the dead, and having passed through this evil journey, humanity will have learned by experience what evil truly is and how mercifully God has acted in redeeming humanity from it.

But humans need, over time, to grow and mature, not only in their individual lives but over the course of human history, in order to become fit for the destiny that God intends, which is union with the divine.

In Irenaeus's view, God initially created Adam and Eve as immature and childlike in their innocence. But humans need, over time, to grow and mature, not only in their individual lives but over the course of human history, in order to become fit for the destiny that God intends, which is union with the divine. This maturation is a complicated matter of transforming our desires from immediate material desires for base, natural ends to a desire for genuine union and communion with God. Humanity's rebellion against God and descent into sin are essential for the fulfillment of this destiny.

Irenaeus is the first thinker in the Christian tradition to offer an account that divides evil into two groups: natural evil, such as earthquakes, plagues, and so on, and moral evil, that is caused by intentional human will. For Irenaeus, moral evil hurts us as much as the people whom we hurt, but in doing so, it causes us to recognize suffering in our world and, ultimately, choose to turn to God. God will not compel us in this; God will simply continue to offer us salvation, and the deeper we get into despair, the more attractive that offer of redemption will seem.

Two points here require further reflection: First, is it true that to be blessed, one must know what it is to be damned? And second, does this account trivialize the reality of evil and suffering? What about those who suffer horrendous evil without having a chance to learn from it? What about an evil such as the Holocaust, which seems wholly out of proportion to any kind of lesson it could communicate to us? How could we gaze into the eyes of the 12 million people who died in the Holocaust and say that their suffering improved their lives? ■

Name to Know

Irenaeus of Lyon (c. 150–c. 202 C.E.). Irenaeus was probably born in Smyrna and raised by Christian parents. During the persecution of Christians by Marcus Aurelius, Irenaeus was imprisoned for his faith, and he eventually became the second bishop of Lyon.

Suggested Reading

Hick, *Evil and the God of Love.*

Irenaeus, "Against Heresies," in *Ante-Nicene Fathers*, vol. 1, *Apostolic Fathers, Justin Martyr, Irenaeus*, Roberts and Donaldson, eds.

Questions to Consider

1. What do you make of Irenaeus's distinction between natural and moral evil? Was Irenaeus correct to describe certain aspects of our existence, such as hunger or pain, as "evil"? And is it important to differentiate between the evil humans cause and the evil we experience independent of human willing?

2. Is it true that Irenaeus's account of evil risks downplaying or trivializing suffering and evil? Can it be true that evil is a necessary step on the way to greater good?

Creation, Evil, and the Fall—Augustine
Lecture 9

> [In doing evil,] I have damaged the web of human relations and affections in ways that have weakened that web, made it thinner, more fragile; I have deprived that web of human relations and affections of being. I have also lessened the soul of that poor child, and also, Augustine will say, ... I have lessened my own soul, as well.

Augustine of Hippo is sometimes called the second founder of the Christian faith, and he is also one of the greatest thinkers in the West of any religious or philosophical persuasion on evil. Augustine was born in North Africa to a Christian mother and a non-Christian father. At the age of 32, he converted to Christianity and later became bishop of the city of Hippo and rose to prominence as a theologian.

Much of the tradition of African Christianity in the late 4th and early 5th centuries is captured in the work of the theologian Tertullian. Tertullian placed responsibility for evil squarely on humans, who were created entirely free to choose good or evil. Along with this simple responsibility comes a simple punishment: After the Fall, humanity suffers evils. Augustine's story of evil is very different. In his view, the Fall is a mystery; punishment in this life is universal but obscurely distributed; and ultimately, God's justice and mercy will be revealed in salvation. Until then, the relationship between the suffering we experience in this life and the reason we deserve that suffering is completely obscure.

In the background of Augustine's thought was his own youthful attachment to a Gnostic popular

Augustine of Hippo (354–430 C.E.) is best known as the great theorist of human interiority.

religion called Manicheanism. This dualist faith embodied a combat-myth picture of the universe: Matter is evil, and spirit is good. In contrast to this view, Augustine, in later life, insisted that matter is good because a good God created all. Here, he affirms the Hebrew Bible as part of the true revelation of God. Good and evil are not metaphysical rivals for Augustine; all that is, insofar as it exists, is good.

To articulate his view, Augustine makes two fundamental claims about sin and evil. The first is that evil is essentially privational, meaning that evil is an irrational swerving from a wholly good creation that deprives that creation of some quality of being. Evil is, ultimately, a "nothing," a nihilation, essentially nothing more than the privation of some fundamentally good reality. The evil of an act is simply how that act lessens existence in some way. There is no "metaphysical substantiality" to evil; there's no rival metaphysical center of power named "evil" that works against God. Augustine believed in demons, but he understood those demons and Satan as rival spirits rebelling against God, though nonetheless under God's sovereign control.

The second claim Augustine makes is sometimes called the perversion theme. If evil is nothing, then sinful people are perverted toward wanting nothing; they are turned away from what they should want and aim their lives at wanting things that are empty, meaningless. Here, sin is the perversion of an originally wholly good human nature. But perversion—human wickedness— ironically always bears the appearance of an intelligible good. For Augustine, any human act has a reason, and he believes it is impossible for someone to want to do evil precisely because it is evil—a radical nihilation.

Despite its dark psychology, Augustine's is a relatively optimistic picture of human behavior. Its sin is merely a perversion of humanity's originally good nature, although that makes it more difficult to eliminate, because those who are caught in the grip of sin often cannot see that what they're doing is bad. But it also means, ironically, that humans have not completely gone astray from the good path because they still think about what they're doing in terms of a good end. Note that evil is not mere "appearance" on this account. In fact, the logic of perversion functions to secure the reality of evil.

In *The Confessions*, Augustine offers an interesting comparison of an evil act he once performed and the crimes of the Roman tyrant Sulla. He says that his own act of stealing pears from a neighbor's tree is worse than the cruelty and savagery of Sulla because his act lacked even the appearance of rationality. Sulla, at least, had material aims—power, wealth—while Augustine merely sought to destroy another's property. This story marks an important moment in the history of thinking about evil: the radical interiorization of evil, the suggestion that the outward manifestation of evil may be somehow less important than what evil does to one's soul. Perhaps even more frightening is the thought that some people don't even try to make sense of the evil they do. Augustine sees a mysterious parallel between that kind of anarchic evil—evil without a beginning, without a rationale—and God's providence. Again, the cost of securing God from responsibility for human evil is to make that evil mysterious. Further, because Augustine focuses on inner evil—the corruption of the inner self as the root of outward misbehavior—he makes evil even more mysterious and, perhaps, more remarkable—as it should be. ■

Despite its dark psychology, Augustine's is a relatively optimistic picture of human behavior.

Name to Know

Augustine of Hippo (354–430 C.E.). Sometimes called the "second founder of the faith," Augustine is commonly recognized as one of the most important figures in Western Christianity. He was born in Thagasate, a Roman city in North Africa.

Suggested Reading

Augustine, *City of God*, Dyson, ed. and trans.

Augustine, *Confessions*, Boulding, trans.

Brown, *Augustine of Hippo: A Biography*.

Evans, *Augustine on Evil*.

1. Do you find Augustine's claim that evil is "privation" convincing? What could it mean to say that evil has no metaphysical reality but is instead a "lessening" or "lack" of reality? Does this view contradict or compliment the early Christian emphasis on apocalyptic conflict?

2. How ought we to assess Augustine's claim that evil is a perversion of a wholly good world? Is evil something alien to the world's true being or something implicit in the world from the very beginning?

3. Does Augustine's story of the pear tree strike you as insightful or exaggerated? Is there such a thing as unmotivated evil?

Rabbinic Judaism—The Evil Impulse
Lecture 10

> I think that there's a deep insight being communicated in especially the Rabbinic tradition's focus on the minutiae of life, the small things around life, simple decency rather than moral heroism. The rabbis' resistance to more theologically radical pictures of evil—like the Christian Satan, for example— ... makes evil an intrinsic part of humans' natural makeup in a certain sense.

The mainstream view in Jewish traditions over the past two millennia is that of **Rabbinic Judaism**. This form of Jewish faith and practice arose in the 1st century in the wake of the destruction of the Temple in Jerusalem and the Diaspora and flourished from the 3rd century until the 20th. Rabbinic Judaism offers a powerful but subtly nuanced picture of evil in wholly mundane terms, one that resists the cosmic drama of sin and redemption found in Christianity.

Much of the discussion in the Rabbinic tradition centers on the "evil" and the "good" impulses in the human heart. The rabbis saw God creating in humans two different and rival sources of energy, with humans caught in a contest between these two competing energies. The Jewish conception of these two impulses suggests an entirely different picture from the Christian one of how the human is organized and what sort of motives and struggles go on inside us.

The good impulse is something like what we would call conscience; it's an inner sense that alerts us when we are considering violating God's law. This impulse develops around age 12 or 13, when Jewish youth first begin to struggle with God's word in Torah and the observance of the Commandments. In contrast, the evil impulse is innate in humans from the womb. This impulse, however, is not demonic; it's not an unnatural expression of some sort of anarchic hostility to God's creation. It seems rooted, rather, in a kind of paranoid self-interest, an expression of the idea that we naturally take special interest in our own well-being and, in many cases, view the world as a threatening place.

Jewish thought seems influenced by a desire to distinguish itself from Christian thinking in its resistance to the overdramatization of evil. For example, it turns out that the "bad" impulse is what enables humans to build houses, to marry, to have children, and to engage in business. It is the source of self-interest, even self-interest properly construed. The danger, of course, is that self-interest can become excessive and overmaster us.

> **Evil is something we meet in our hearts and our lives every day. It is a challenge and a gift sent by God to bring humans to maturity.**

The implication of this psychology for understanding the human condition is that humans are caught up not so much in a vast metaphysical melodrama as they are in trying to handle temptations encountered every day. For the rabbis, evil is not supernatural but derived from our naturally created being; it is something that happens to us because of our impulses. Unlike many popular Christian accounts—in which the devil is a powerful presence in the world, seducing humans—in this account, evil's origins are sought in the exercise of the human will.

This view doesn't trivialize evil because when it is left uncountered by other parts of our nature, the evil impulse can lead us astray and cause great damage. The Rabbinic view recognizes this impulse as powerful; it's a life force, but it can warp us in ways that are against life. Its power is related to its initial appearance as small; it moves in subtle ways. As the Talmud puts it, "At first the evil impulse is called a 'wayfarer,' then it is called a 'guest,' then finally it is called a 'master.'" In this account, evil is not so much an abstract philosophical problem as it is a practical challenge confronting those afflicted by it. It is something we meet in our hearts and our lives every day. It is a challenge and a gift sent by God to bring humans to maturity. This is part of a larger understanding of the nature of Jewish suffering: Evil serves as a challenge but not one that will overwhelm the people Israel.

The Rabbinic account is a profound challenge to an overly Christianized conception of evil in light of sin. Indeed, this picture is so different from Christian notions of evil that some Jewish scholars consider it a picture of "badness" rather than "evil." This tradition emphasizes human responsibility and struggle, especially the struggle to live in accordance with Jewish law.

This account is not, however, without its problems, especially for Jews living since the Holocaust, the **Shoah** ("catastrophe"). Is this picture of evil too mundane and too ordinary to handle the Shoah? Ironically, the Shoah may threaten any account of evil that is *not* vastly dramatic. The evil for the rabbis is about greed, jealously, envy; it's a happy and relatively small-scale picture of evil. This picture seems not to be continuous with the evil that was experienced in the Holocaust—evil completely out of proportion to the character of everyday moral challenges. When the Holocaust occurred, many believed that the longstanding covenant between God and God's people had fallen apart. God let the Holocaust happen, and since that time, Jews have been struggling to understand the meaning of the Shoah. ■

Important Terms

Rabbinic Judaism: Form of Jewish faith and practice that flourished from the 3rd century C.E., the era of the composition of the Talmud, to the present.

Shoah: Hebrew word meaning "catastrophe," now often used to describe the Holocaust.

Suggested Reading

Urbach, *The Sages: The World and Wisdom of the Rabbis of the Talmud*, Abrahams, trans.

Questions to Consider

1. What advantages does the more mundane understanding of evil in Judaism hold over the Christian view? What are its drawbacks?

2. How do you assess the rabbis' understanding of *yetzer ha ra* (the bad impulse) and *vetzer ha tov* (the good impulse)? Do human beings naturally possess both good and evil impulses? Or, perhaps, is *yetzer ha ra* even a necessary part of human flourishing?

Islam—Iblis the Failed, Once-Glorious Being
Lecture 11

The Qur'an is unique among the Scriptures of the Abrahamic faiths in explicitly rendering the episode of the origin of evil in creation by recounting the rebellion of Iblis, the rebellious spirit. Some Islamic thinkers call Iblis an angel; some call Iblis a genie. Iblis is the one who becomes Ash Shaitan, the primordial rebel against God.

Islamic conceptions are relevant to a Western understanding of evil for a number of reasons, not least of which is that Islam serves, in a way, like Rabbinic Judaism: as a kind of internal critic of mainstream Western thinking about evil.

The **Qur'an** is the sacred text of Islam, but it is not, per se, the Muslim Bible. In a way that is different from the Torah and the Christian New and Old Testaments, the Qur'an itself is sacramental, a material means of holiness, a way of participating in God. It is, in some sense, more akin to the Christian Eucharist than to the Christian Bible or the Jewish Torah. Further, in Islam, there is no distance between the content of God's message and the poetic and linguistic form in which it exists in the Qur'an. This recitation is exactly what God meant to give God's people.

The Qur'an tells the story of **Iblis**, the rebellious spirit, who is asked by God to "bow down to Adam." But Iblis refuses to do so, and God is angered. Iblis tells God, "I will lay in wait for them, everywhere, on Your straight path." God replies, "You who were once high, now I am casting you down low."

The main traditions of interpreting this story cast light on Islamic understandings of evil and the relation between religious piety and moral rectitude. Augustine would point out that Iblis has motives for his refusal of God: It seems inappropriate that he should lower himself below Adam, who is made of clay, given that Iblis was made of fire. Note, too, that Iblis does not act; he refuses to act. Then, in his description of why he will now lay in wait for the good people of God, Iblis says, "Because you, God, brought me low." It seems that evil can be both something that is done by people and something that happens to them, and in fact, many people who have done evil acts report their deeds as things they were compelled to do. The action looks ambivalently as if it was done and as if it happened, as if it didn't really have an agent.

Further, in the Islamic tradition, Satan himself is only ambiguously a personal agent. Sometimes Iblis appears as an agent, a person, with desires and designs on humanity, but at other times Iblis seems more like an impersonal force, a power in the cosmos that humans experience as preying on their weaknesses and seducing them. But is it they who convince themselves that they are seduced, much in the way that Iblis convinced himself that it was God who cast him down? Such questions of responsibility are enormously complicated. The idea here seems to be that evil is both personal and impersonal at once—both something you do and something you watch yourself doing.

The Qur'an is the revelation according to Muhammad. It was written in pieces during Muhammad's life. Then it was compiled, organized, and fixed textually after his death.

This also helps us think about Iblis as saturating all dimensions of human existence. Satan is potentially everywhere and anywhere, in all of our deficiencies, large and small. But most fundamental of all in this account is the fact that Iblis doesn't do anything. He is committed in the most literal way to nothing.

The majority tradition in Islamic thought thus gives us a powerful and stark depiction of Iblis as a failed creature, a once-glorious being now fallen into a darkness of the soul. But another tradition, one represented by a number of Sufi mystics, suggests that Iblis was, in a certain way, the perfect monotheist, the one angel who would not bow down and worship Adam when God created him. These writers suggest that even monotheism can be taken too far, that it can become a kind of idolatry, and that the believer can become, in a certain sense, holier than thou. Judaism and Christianity, too, recognize that it is always possible to misappropriate the faith. Simply being a believer is no guarantee of moral rectitude; in fact, the appearance of belief can itself be one of the best disguises for evil.

For the Sufis and those who follow them, this interpretation of Iblis is part of a larger mystical worldview in which all is in God's hands. God's will for Iblis is not violated by Iblis's refusal to bow before humanity but fulfilled by it. This interpretation insinuates a complication into the main story that offers an even deeper insight into the nature of evil. Evil's origin is not completely irrational, nor simply a matter of excessive self-love or a sense of pride; evil is due to a misplaced but plausible sense of right value. This leads us to think about the ways in which our own traditions might not just enable but perhaps aggravate or amplify evil. ■

Important Terms

Iblis: Rebellious angel in the Qur'an, later associated with Satan.

Qur'an: Sacred text of Islam, literally meaning the "recitation." Contains the revelation according to Muhammad, transmitted to him by Gabriel.

Suggested Reading

Awn, *Satan's Tragedy and Redemption: Iblis in Sufi Psychology*.

Questions to Consider

1. Recall the concluding question of this lecture in light of the discussion of Iblis in Islamic thought: Might evil itself be, at least sometimes, prompted by a genuine good? What do you think the answer to this is?

2. Does the understanding of Iblis offered by Sufism present Satan too sympathetically? Or are we right to see evil as, in some sense, more of a tragic mistake than a malicious occurrence?

3. How does the Islamic account of Iblis illuminate Jewish and Christian conceptions of Satan and evil? Does the contrast make the unique aspects of each tradition more striking?

On Self-Deception in Evil—Scholasticism
Lecture 12

What does evil feel like, or more accurately, what does it think like, from inside? This is a profound and interesting effort at empathy toward something that we really shouldn't feel empathy toward, not because Augustine and those who followed him, like Aquinas, wanted to feel pity for wicked-doers, but rather, because they wanted to get as clear as possible about the inner logic of evil's rationales.

This lecture shifts us back from Islamic to Christian thinking, in particular, the Scholasticism that emerged in Western monastic schools starting soon after the end of the 1st millennium. This style of teaching and learning involved mastering a huge body of traditional theological information, developing the ability to summarize that information and articulate it in potent expressions, and debating the various tensions and conflicts that emerged from within that body of knowledge. This focus on debating the details of Christian theology demanded a precise and intricate kind of reasoning. Two of the greatest thinkers in the Scholastic tradition were Anselm of Lyon and **Thomas Aquinas**, both of whom chose to concentrate their study of the nature of evil on the fallen angels—the devil and his minions—rather than humans. In this lecture, we'll look at the "logic" of Satan's rebellion through the thought of Anselm and what we might call the "moral psychology" of the devil and communal evil through the works of Aquinas.

Thomas Aquinas (1225–1274) is often considered the greatest mind in the scholastic age.

In his very brief treatise "On the Fall of the Devil," Anselm explores the nature of Satan's motivation for rebelling against God's providential order, unpacks the multiple dimensions of misery that befell Satan because of that rebellion, and offers a picture of the relationship between good and evil in the cosmos. Much of the treatise in general can be summarized in the pithy statement of Anselm that Satan wanted everything and got nothing, while the good angels sought nothing and received everything.

Aquinas's description illuminates the nature of human evil and the curious collegiality it can provoke in its adherents.

For Anselm, the pursuit of one's own good without reliance on God or anyone else is both radically self-deceptive about one's identity as a creature of God and about one's true good, namely, loving dependence and relation, a sharing in God's community. God created the universe and gave all the creatures within it a will to participate in the universe, but Anselm says, each of the creatures must actualize that will—inhabit and endorse it. The mystery of the devil is that he inexplicably chooses not to accept that will and seeks something more; what that "more" is can't be specified. The devil's desire is bottomless; because it can never be specified, it can never be sated, and the fact of this longing is what makes Satan miserable.

The work of Aquinas offers, perhaps, a less dense picture of the mindset of an evildoer. What does a wicked person's mind report to itself when it is doing evil? Aquinas gives us a wonderful description of what he thinks it was like for Satan to have convinced himself that he was going to succeed in rebelling against God. Aquinas believed that Satan wanted to be like God, not because he wanted to be separate from God—that would be the same as saying that he didn't want to exist—but because he desired "something he could attain by the virtue of his own nature, turning his appetite away from the supernatural beatitude which is obtained by God's grace." Satan believes it's possible, in other words, to keep the end of ultimate happiness in his mind as an ideal that he will try to attain, but he also convinces himself that he can get it by his own efforts, rather than receiving it as a gift from God.

In this, Aquinas explains Satan's motivations for rebelling against God: There's a resentment that God is higher than Satan and a desire to be like

God, both slathered over with self-deception, the ability of Satan to convince himself that he can get to what God is. This also explains the nature of the allegiance the infernal creatures make with one another. The fallen angels work together, but each pursues his own solitary ends; each one wants to be his own God. Aquinas's description illuminates the nature of human evil and the curious collegiality it can provoke in its adherents.

For Augustine, Anselm, and Aquinas, evil is, most of all, privative; it deprives reality of being in some ways, and it does this by shrinking back from connection to the rest of reality. Evil is an attempt to be private, and for Aquinas and these other thinkers, that notion of radical solitude is theologically problematic. This idea is interesting in comparison to our world, where we value privacy deeply. Nonetheless, Anselm and Aquinas give us deep, realistic, and profound pictures of the role of self-deception in the exercise and agency of evil. ■

Name to Know

Aquinas, Thomas (1225–1274 C.E.). Born to a prominent family in Aquino in southern Italy. At the age of 19, Aquinas expressed a desire to join the monastic order of the Dominicans, but his family opposed this decision and locked him in a castle for two years.

Suggested Reading

Anselm, *Anselm of Canterbury: The Major Works*, Davies and Evans, eds.

Aquinas, *On Evil*, Davies, ed., Regan, trans.

———, *Summa Theologiae*, Fathers of the American Dominican Province, trans.

1. What do you make of the Scholastic attempt to understand evil by dwelling on the fall of Satan and the angels? Does this approach seem clarifying or obscuring?

2. Is Aquinas right to suggest that evil may often involve self-deception and the desire to attain something that one simply cannot possess? What are some examples of this kind of self-deception common in our world?

Dante—Hell and the Abandonment of Hope
Lecture 13

The most direct historical implication of this passage is very disquieting, and that is, of course, that the gate to Auschwitz in the Holocaust had over it a sign, as well, and that sign said, "*Arbeit macht frei*," "Work will make you free." Clearly, that sign was modeled on Dante's *Inferno* sign.

Dante Alighieri's vision of hell in his epic poem the *Inferno* has probably done more to shape Western imaginations of hell, the devil, and punishment than any other work. In this lecture, we'll look at three themes in the poem: the overall logic of hell; the paradoxical logic of what Dante calls the ***contrapasso***, the "counter-penalty," on which the nature of punishment in hell is based; and the ultimate irony that is at the heart of the poem.

The *Inferno* is the first part of Dante's *Divine Comedy*, a story of a man who is facing a crisis of faith and identity and is taught the true nature of reality in guided tours of hell, purgatory, and paradise. Most people read the *Inferno* for its depiction of hell, but the real story of the poem is the moral and spiritual development of the character Dante, who is reported as growing in wisdom throughout the *Divine Comedy*. We see, for example, his changing

Dante Alighieri (c. 1265–1321) is one of the most powerful describers of evil in the Christian tradition.

understanding of the word *pietá*, which means both "piety" and "pity." Dante meets adulterers, deceivers, murderers, and others on his journey; the details of their crimes differ, but they all share one thing in common: They never owned up to what they had done or what they had become. True piety in this situation is to have no pity for the damned; it is to see and judge the damned as God sees and judges them.

To understand what Dante learns in the course of his journey, we have to understand the nature of infernal punishment and the logic of *contrapasso*, "counter-punishment": the way in which each person's punishment perfectly fits his or her defining crime. Indeed, each punishment is a kind of cryptogram that must be decoded by Dante—and us—in order to see the moral reality it represents.

Each punishment is a kind of cryptogram that must be decoded by Dante—and us—in order to see the moral reality it represents.

The most famous lines in the poem are those on the sign above the gates of hell: "Before me nothing was created / that was not eternal, and I endure eternally. / Abandon every hope, you who enter." It's interesting to consider Satan's position with regard to these lines. He is trapped in the ice in a frozen lake at the bottom of hell, but when Dante and Virgil climb out of hell after observing Satan, we find that, in fact, hell is upside down from the perspective of the rest of reality. From the soles of Satan's feet, Dante and Virgil look up and see the Mount of Paradise, on top of which rests God. In other words, Satan is locked in the ice, and he's not just trying to escape the ice; he's still trying to get away from God. In some sense, he is condemning himself to hell by his own activity.

Hell is not extrinsic to the crimes for which the damned are sent there. When Dante saw the adulterous lovers in hell, he felt pity for them. But in refusing to own up to what they had done, the lovers are saying that they don't want to be around God; they don't want to be around the truth. Hell is an extension of the crimes of the damned, their full flowering. Hell is what evil wants to be.

Satan wants more than anything else not to serve God. But everything that is, including Satan, is part of God's system. Thus, Satan's real desire is, in some way, not to be at all. Still, because Satan is a creature of God and finds his own being good, he cannot but want to persevere in that being. Satan's most essential desire—not to be a part of God's creation—conflicts with the foundations of his own essential being; he wants to be and not be at the same time.

Remember that every punishment is a cryptogram of the sin that it punishes. What was the real sin of Satan? His desire to escape God's service. The thing that would turn that sin against itself is to serve as the lynchpin of hell, to become the vehicle whereby God makes hell. Satan's sin is to desire not to serve God, and his punishment is precisely to become one of God's greatest servants. We can go one step further and note that it is the beating of his own wings that keeps Satan trapped in the ice. This reveals the irony in the sign above the gate at the entrance. "Abandon all hope, you who enter" doesn't mean "Just give up now"; it means get over your false hopes, leave your "spin" behind, and you might be able to leave. If you want out of hell, all you have to do is give up hope of getting yourself out. Hell is ultimately self-made and self-inflicted; it's chosen by the damned themselves. ∎

Name to Know

Alighieri, Dante (c. 1265–1321 C.E.). Born in Florence, Italy, to a prominent family. Like many of his contemporaries, Dante was thoroughly involved in the controversy between the Guelphs and the Ghibellines, two factions associated with the papacy and the Holy Roman Empire in a struggle for political prominence.

Important Term

contrapasso: Theme in Dante's *Inferno* that emphasizes the continuity between sin and punishment in hell.

Suggested Reading

Dante, *Inferno*, Hollander and Hollander, trans.

Hawkins, *Dante: A Brief History*.

1. Was Dante right in his assertion that we ought not pity the damned? Does true piety also entail a refusal to pity those who are punished for their evil deeds?

2. How would you respond to Dante's suggestion that hell may be an intrinsic (rather than extrinsic) punishment? Is it true that evil often does contain its own punishment and that perhaps hell is the fullest expression of this?

The Reformation—The Power of Evil Within
Lecture 14

The proper theological term for what Calvin believed in and affirmed is a "super-lapsarian double predestination." That's a pretty impressive thing; it sounds like, again, something you'd expect an Olympic gymnast to do or something.

In this lecture, we move into the Reformation and the boundaries of the modern world. The two thinkers we'll encounter, **Martin Luther** and **Jean Calvin**, are influenced by the past but also profoundly innovative and, in some ways, set the terms for much that will come.

The Reformation emerged amid increasing concern about the stability of the created order. Massive social change—the beginnings of an industrial revolution and a booming economy—had occurred in the wake of the devastation of the Black Death. Intellectually, people were beginning to develop new ways to understand and organize society and the cosmos.

The thinking of Martin Luther grew out of anxieties related to the individual's relationship to God in this age of social change. For Luther, the church was a secondary expression of this relationship. He believed that God is absolutely powerful and completely sovereign but mysteriously hidden from us. All we have is the God visible in the Scriptures and in Jesus Christ. The distance between the human Christ and the all-powerful God is the space in which the devil plays with us. The devil, for Luther, is an inner power, able to corrupt faith. He is immaterial, but he obstructs and mystifies humans into making terrible choices. And he is most interested in striking at those who are serious about being good Christians.

One of the most important concepts in Luther's thinking is "works righteousness"; this is the idea that we are made good by what we do, that in some sense, we have to earn or deserve our salvation. The devil loves this idea, insofar as he can insinuate it into our minds: that we would have anything to do with our salvation and, thus, could claim any credit for our salvation. For Luther, the response we should use when confronted with the temptation to think this way is simple: Instead of trying to fight the devil ourselves, we must appeal to Christ to protect us.

The picture of evil that Luther offers is not one of threat or immediate danger; it is, rather, of deception and obscurity. To counteract evil, Luther insists on the absolute governance of the world by a sovereign and providential deity. God's providential mastery over creation is so important to Luther that he's willing to ascribe a responsibility for evil to God. To explain this responsibility, he appeals to the idea of the inscrutability of divine providence, the lives of Abraham and Job, and the prophetic tradition's interpretation of the travails of ancient Israel. Any attempt to master God's providential control over history on our part will fail. Direct, immediate resistance to evil is a collapse into evil itself, because it returns us to relying on ourselves.

Martin Luther (1483–1546) was a trained medieval scholastic, versed in the thought of Aquinas and Anselm.

The thinking of Jean Calvin presents a very different picture. Calvin is famous for his ideas of predestination and the total depravity of humanity. He believed that the blessed are predestined to heaven and the damned are predestined to hell, and they are both predestined in those ways from before the Fall. In other words, before humans fell, God foreknew and preordained—not just knew but determined—that some would be blessed and some would be damned. This doctrine of election means that everything about you is outside of your immediate control. This is good news for Calvin precisely because of the doctrine of total depravity.

Calvin believes that human nature was changed—deranged—in the Fall, but it's not evil. Humans are trapped in sin, but they are not actually compelled to sin; our desires are so warped that we actually want to sin. This means that without God's providential control over our lives, we are certain to send ourselves to hell. It is only the mysterious, gracious providence of God's love

Lecture 14: The Reformation—The Power of Evil Within

© Photos.com/Thinkstock.

that allows any of us to be corrected from our own completely idolatrous ways to move toward salvation. For Calvin, unlike Luther, there's very little active place for Satan in this thinking. The human mind itself does more than enough to make evil happen in the world.

What happens in the Christian life to resist Calvin's picture of drowning in sin is sanctification. This is the practice whereby those Christians who have been saved come ever more fully to live their lives as holy people. Evil resists sanctification because evil is slothful, narcissistic, and inward-turning; sanctification is an increasing direction of our energy outward to one another and to God. We must not do anything but understand ourselves as redeemed by God, and part of that redemption is a renunciation of our own perpetual efforts to hide from our reality. Christians are not free from sin for Calvin; in fact, they are never more sensible of sin, their own and others, than when they have been saved. ∎

Names to Know

Calvin, Jean (1509–1564 C.E.). Calvin was born in France and studied philosophy and law. He was strongly influenced by French humanism and was eventually forced to flee France because of his call for Catholic reforms.

Luther, Martin (1483–1546 C.E.). Born in Eisleben, Germany, a city that was then part of the Holy Roman Empire. Luther briefly studied law but became a monk in the Augustinian order after making a vow during a lightning storm.

Suggested Reading

Calvin, *Institutes of the Christian Religion*, McNeill, ed., Battles, trans.

Gordon, *Calvin*.

Luther, *Basic Theological Writings*, Lull, Russell, and Pelikan, eds.

Obermann, *Luther: Man between God and the Devil*, Walliser-Schwarzbart, trans.

1. As noted in the lecture, the thinkers of the Reformation did not emerge out of thin air; rather, their innovations concerning the nature of evil were thoroughly related to their historical experience of dislocation, disease, and change. What analogous historical or cultural experiences are shaping our current conceptions of evil?

2. For Luther, the devil was profoundly powerful, though utterly immaterial. Do you agree with Luther that evil is always tempting but never compelling? Can the devil ever "make" someone do anything?

3. Calvin famously argued that all aspects of creation—including evil itself—exist under God's providential governance. Does this emphasis on governance risk making God too complicit in evil? How can God allow but not endorse evil?

Dark Politics—Machiavelli on How to Be Bad
Lecture 15

The central aim is stability, but you have to understand people's psychologies—how they resent things and how to quiet those resentments—not because you want them to like you, but because you don't want them to render the political community unstable.

With this lecture, we move into more secular approaches to the question of evil. Here, God looks very far away at best, and morality may be real but only a small part of the world that we inhabit.

Niccolo Machiavelli is a famous figure but often misunderstood. He notoriously said, "The prince must love his city more than his soul" and, in order to love his city correctly, must learn how not to be good. Machiavelli seems to be the first person to think that the reality of evil in politics is inescapable and that the prince, instead of trying to resist it, should, at certain points and in certain ways, work with the grain of politics rather than against it in favor of a larger moral aim.

Machiavelli is often thought of as a relativist, a nihilist, a man who counseled mendacity, duplicity, skulduggery, and a bloody-minded malfeasance to politicians. Although Machiavelli himself would not have been entirely displeased to have his works become camouflaged by that reputation, for those who read him carefully, another and more profound meaning emerges. His basic idea is that goodness and virtue are real but that moral perfection cannot provide any simple guidelines for the governance of our world, especially in politics. This is why the prince or any political ruler must learn how not to be good.

Machiavelli believes that a prince is wise to punish rebels against the realm even after they have surrendered, primarily because their punishment will deter others from undertaking similar rebellions. Fear is an important political motivator. Even more controversially, Machiavelli recommends the use of proxies for especially unpleasant deeds, proxies whom the prince can later turn on and punish for performing those very deeds. This approach defuses the resentments of the citizenry by directing them to a suitable target, who can then be properly punished, avoiding future instability in the realm. The integrity of a political agenda is, for Machiavelli, the absolute baseline for a successful political regime.

This line of thinking represents a significant change from earlier political treatises, which first and foremost, exhorted rulers to be good and moral. For Machiavelli, this is simply unrealistic, both in terms of what is possible for political rulers and because it mistakes the cause and effect of certain actions in the polity. A nice and decent ruler may seem weak to some people; a just ruler may be unable to defuse the resentment of those who were against his getting into power. Thus, a simple moralism in politics may be against the good of the polis.

Machiavelli believes that people are governed by two broad categories of motivation in politics: their loves and their fears—and primarily the latter.

The central political anxiety for Machiavelli is instability. We must be able to ensure stability in the world for any of the other goods of politics or private life to go forward. This means that the stability of the political order must come before the ethical happiness of that order. Politics is extremely complicated. How can we anticipate that morality will result in some useful system with which to govern the lives of the citizens when we can't ensure that everyone agrees about what's right and wrong? In fact, we know that politics inevitably generates different judgments from different people. Simply telling people that they ought to be good sets politicians up to lose.

Machiavelli believes that people are governed by two broad categories of motivation in politics: their loves and their fears—and primarily the latter. Rulers, he says, can rely on the idea that people are much more likely to do things if they are frightened by concrete threats than if they are offered vague hopes of good things in the future. Machiavelli also believes that *fortuna*, "fortune" or "luck," plays a significant role in politics. In this realm, luck or accident might take the form of an economic crisis or a military threat. Such events are not in the ruler's control, yet he is responsible for facing them, and at times, he may have to take unpleasant actions to secure the good of the community. Much of this is read as strategies for being a wicked ruler, but Machiavelli is not trying to teach people how to be evil. Rather, he says that the most powerful medicine against the prince's corruption is his ability to control situations where unpleasant actions must be undertaken. Machiavelli wants to teach rulers how to be evil in a cold-blooded way so that the evil doesn't infect them and make them entirely hot-blooded evildoers. This is why being a prince is so difficult; a prince must make a stone of his heart.

Machiavelli advocates a certain cold-eyed realism about the political world, but his thinking also speaks to us of the need to resist pretty ideas. For Machiavelli, politics is the art of the possible, not the art of the ideal. ∎

Name to Know

Machiavelli, Niccolo (1469–1527 C.E.). Born in Florence, Italy, where he received a classical education and training in service to the Florentine state.

Suggested Reading

Machiavelli, *The Portable Machiavelli*, Bonadella and Musa, eds.

Skinner, *Machiavelli: A Very Brief Introduction*.

Questions to Consider

1. Do we expect our rulers to be "bad" for the sake of our polity? Was Machiavelli right to insist that a ruler ought not be good but, rather, be willing to do wrong for the sake of his or her country?

2. Do you read Machiavelli's position as a "realistic" or a pessimistic one? Should we expect that virtue and politics go well together or not?

3. How do we see Machiavelli's ideas at work in the contemporary world of politics?

Hobbes—Evil as a Social Construct
Lecture 16

> Given ... that moral norms arise from peoples' cooperation to affirm laws and rules—whether explicit rules about right and wrong in the form of political laws, traffic laws, etc., or tacit rules about what is good or bad behavior in the form of cultural standards— ... the state of humans in the state of nature means, for Hobbes, that in nature itself, there are no such standards; there are no such laws.

Thomas Hobbes is generally considered to be the first truly modern philosopher in Western history. His great work *Leviathan* is relevant for us in two important ways: First, in his overall picture of humans in a state of nature, he seems to suggest that evil is the human's natural state. Second, he insists that good and evil are not metaphysically natural categories; they're not descriptions of reality but essentially constituted by the constructed political community in which we live.

The "state of nature" is a complicated condition that Hobbes uses to imagine what people would be like outside of civilization. In this condition, humans are roughly equal in strength and intelligence, that is, in their hope of being able to get what they want. They are also roughly equal in fear. Humans in a state of nature seek to fulfill their basic needs and are naturally fearful of others because they know that each one of them could kill another. For Hobbes, this results in a permanent state of semi-conflict: the "war of all against all." No one in this situation can be trusted because there is no way of holding another to account if trust is violated. These conditions engender a spiraling paranoia in humans: There is always good reason to harm someone else, even if you have no evidence that he is going to harm you, because he could harm you at some point in the future. For Hobbes, if we want to put in place a stable system of government, we can't begin from a sense of humanity's decency or kindness; we must acknowledge this savagery.

Hobbes is not saying that humans are naturally evil; in fact, outside of some preset social order, he believes there is no way to talk about good and evil at all. The savagery of humans when left to their devices suggests that morality has no reality as a metaphysical standard or a natural motivator for humans. In the state of nature, there are no moral norms. "The Desires," Hobbes writes, "are in themselves no Sin. No more are the Actions ... till they know a law that forbids them: which till lawes be made they cannot know." Without laws, people don't know or care if they're doing right or wrong; they're doing what is, strictly speaking, in their own interest.

To counteract this state of complete moral anarchy and amoralism, humans collectively agree to work together. Most of what we know of life, including our apprehension of good and evil, derives from this decision to live in communities. For Hobbes, good and evil literally have no reference beyond our agreement on these categories. Morality has no basis in our natures but is merely something we construct socially.

Absent that strong ruler and a very narrow range of principles, human life will devolve again into being "solitary, poor, nasty, brutish, and short."

In their readings of Thucydides, Hobbes and his contemporaries realized that language itself has the ability to be mobile across meanings and that sometimes changes in language may be the result of changing political circumstances. Hobbes goes even further than this: Not only can language be perverted by politics, but absent politics, language loses its sense altogether.

Nonetheless, human flourishing relies on successful human communities and use of language, and the conditions under which such communities can be founded and can continue through time are very narrow. Typically for Hobbes, these conditions involve a powerful, almost tyrannical, executive power to ensure obedience. Absent that strong ruler and a very narrow range of principles, human life will devolve again into being "solitary, poor, nasty, brutish, and short." In all of this, Hobbes is merely describing the conditions of humans, not endorsing the view that morality is just convention. He certainly thought that any ethical system, once established, ought to be obeyed to avoid reverting to the state of nature.

Many people have challenged Hobbes's views, both about the nature of human motivation in a state of nature and about whether morality exists outside of social conventions. Joseph Butler, an Anglican bishop, challenged the core premise of Hobbes's picture of moral psychology by pointing to the phenomenology of moral experience—the experience a person has when he or she is doing something good or bad. Butler argued that humans act out of two different senses of self-interest: the desire to accomplish our own aims and the desire to express genuine caring for others. Butler's assertion that Hobbes misunderstood human moral psychology is still debated today, and Hobbes's picture of rational self-interest has influenced modern game theory in its aim to apply mathematical models to the interactions of people and nations. ■

Name to Know

Hobbes, Thomas (1588–1679 C.E.). Born in Wiltshire, England—supposedly when his mother heard news of the first sighting of the Spanish Armada—and educated at Oxford.

Suggested Reading

Hobbes, *Leviathan*, Tuck, ed.

Hobbes, trans., *The Peloponnesian War*, Grene, ed.

Martinich, *Hobbes: A Biography*.

Questions to Consider

1. For Hobbes, talking about evil only made sense in a social context—good and evil are culturally constructed, not "naturally" present in the world. What role does communal agreement play in identifying what is good and evil? Are good and evil primarily categories that humans create in communities or essences naturally present in the world?

2. What is human existence like in the "state of nature"? Is a strong centralized authority necessary to defend humans against chaos?

Montaigne and Pascal—Evil and the Self
Lecture 17

A lot of these people coming out of the Renaissance focus on this Renaissance theme of the creativity, ... but whereas other Renaissance thinkers seem to think that is an unremittingly positive thing about the human, thinkers that we've been looking at—Calvin, Montaigne, Pascal—they all identify the turbulence of the mind as one of the most profound modern innovations when it comes to thinking about the roots of evil.

O ur thinkers in this lecture, Montaigne and Pascal, engage in a debate about the intricate connections among religious belief, the self, and the self's performance of its beliefs in the world. Most centrally for both thinkers, the main question is about the dangers of zealotry (Montaigne) or the dangers of a lack of zealotry (Pascal).

Michel de Montaigne was a profound student of the effects of our beliefs on others, particularly how our beliefs may cause others to suffer great evil. He lived in an age of hyper-zealotry, though he did not share in that zealotry. His book *Essais* was the product of 10 years of near-total isolation from his family and others. One theme that emerges throughout the *Essais* is the tension between the vehemence of one's beliefs and the reality of the world's apparent indifference to those beliefs and the way those beliefs can lead to horrific suffering on the part of others.

In the *Essais*, Montaigne focuses on the banalities of everyday life, an activity that he thinks teaches us more than attention to abstract dogmas or doctrines of philosophical theories. Through these banalities, we discover how we actually behave, and we learn that humans are completely ramshackle assemblages of desires, interests, and thoughts; more or less coherent but fundamentally misaligned within ourselves. To try to fix this messiness, Montaigne suggests, leads inevitably to evil, although our inherent creativity often results in anti-humane, anti-worldly beliefs and behaviors.

In a number of essays, Montaigne analyzes the ways in which zealous, hyper-sincere piety can be destructive on its own or can curdle into a kind of hatred that is even more evil than its direct expression would be. In an essay titled "Of Virtue," he cites a number of gruesome stories—of self-mutilation, suicide, and martyrdom—all connected by the thread of extremity. In another essay, "Of Moderation," Montaigne asserts that nature, including human nature, is moderate, but the human mind need not be moderate. This is our glory and our tragedy: Our imagination is so fertile that we are prone to thoughts that can lead to annihilation of ourselves and others. We have this tendency because we prefer simple answers and final solutions to our own messiness.

Another voice in this conversation is that of the mathematician and scientist Blaise Pascal. In philosophy, Pascal is most well known for his *Pensées*, *"Thoughts."* This is a collection of aphorisms that he hoped to organize into an argument for the truth of Christianity. In the *Pensées*, Pascal proves himself to be a great anatomist of the dimensions of self-deception that are pervasive in evil.

For Michel de Montaigne (1533–1592), the main question is about the danger of zealotry, of serious religious belief.

Pascal on evil is classically Augustinian. He is most interested in the cruelty we do to ourselves by not thinking about our religious beliefs. He disagreed with Montaigne profoundly about the relationship between serious religious belief and moral sanity. Where Montaigne saw zealotry as dangerous, for Pascal, anything less than zealotry would be an evasion of the realities confronting us.

Like Montaigne, Pascal saw humans as muddied, but he believed that we were not meant to be in this state. Pascal said that we are "neither an angel nor a beast"; we're filled with "astonishing contradictions"; and we posses "no truth which is either abiding or fully satisfactory." We are moving constantly, both in our minds and in the world, trying to make sense of things and finding no stable resting place. The endlessness of our own perversity teaches us something about the infinitude of our longing: It can be sated only by the presence of God in our lives.

The first step in our healing is a recognition that our lives our riddled with sin and an acknowledgment of the emptiness of so much of what we do. Only with this recognition will the infinite abyss of longing in our hearts be filled by the infinite gift of God. We face difficulty in this because of two warring instincts: We want an end, but we don't want to reflect on ourselves wanting that end. We want to actively avoid thinking about ourselves. Pascal diagnoses this active ignorance with a single devastating word: *divertissements*, "diversions." Our lives are a series of diversions, endless rounds of empty frivolities, that add up to avoidance of confrontation with the basic realities of our existence, most centrally, the fact of our inevitable death. Great evil, Pascal thinks, can come from such trivialities. Pascal believes that people must finally confront the question of whether or not they will believe in God and follow God's commands for them; *divertissement* allows us to avoid this. This is why zealotry is so necessary for Pascal and why he opposes Montaigne's suspicion of it: We must be serious, because in the end, life will come for us and so will death. ∎

Important Term

divertissements: Term meaning "diversions" used by Blaise Pascal to describe a way of being in the world aimed at avoiding the facts of one's existence, especially the fact of death.

Suggested Reading

Connor, *Pascal's Wager: The Man Who Played Dice with God.*

Friedrich, *Montaigne*, Eng, trans., Desan, ed.

Montaigne, *The Complete Essays*, Screech, ed. and trans.

Pascal, *Pensées and Other Writings*, Krailsheimer, ed. and trans.

1. In many ways, Montaigne and Pascal represent two significantly different perspectives on the nature of human existence and the nature of evil. Is diversity and incoherence simply part of human life, or is this itself a product of evil?

2. How would you assess Pascal's observation "It is being miserable to know that one is miserable; but it is also being great to know that one is miserable"? How could knowing one's misery be both debasing and glorifying?

3. Do you agree with Pascal that *divertissement* represents a significant temptation in human life? Can we avoid "wagering" in Pascal's sense or not?

Milton—Epic Evil
Lecture 18

Satan is both simultaneously a rebel and a person who knows rebellion is futile, and the amplitude and magnitude of his verbal rebellion, and the magnificence of it, are paralleled in Milton's representation by a brilliant representation of Satan as also, behind that verbal pomposity, completely despairing about the futility of this whole exercise.

One thinker who potentially rivals Dante for the depth of the influence of his literary work on our thinking about the nature of evil is **John Milton**. The work for which he is best known is ***Paradise Lost***, written, as the poem says, "to justify the ways of God to man." The epic provides us with a powerful depiction of both the character of temptation and the descent into sin and corruption.

Dante wrote about an ordinary person coming to see evil for what it is. In contrast, Milton wrote about evil's self-understanding. And to do that, he bends metaphors in complicated ways, famously describing hell, for example, as "darkness visible." With these paradoxical metaphors, Milton recalls the medieval Christian concept of *felix culpa*, the "happy fault," the view that the Fall of humans was, in some ways, fortuitous because it brought Christ as the savior.

The poem quickly establishes that Satan's sin is rebellion against God, but Satan sees his rebellion as prompted by God and is unwilling to own up to his responsibility. Interestingly, the poem depicts Satan as a master of possibilities, of hypotheticals, but never able to settle on any of them. His language reveals him to be a sinuous thinker. It's also true that Satan oscillates wildly on the question of choice. When he thinks about his own condition, he blames God, but when he thinks about his ambitions, he believes himself to be wholly unsponsored. Satan sees Adam and Eve as innocents, caught up in the war between God and himself. He believes that he is using the tree of the knowledge of good and evil as bait for Adam and Eve, but of course, that turns out not to be the case. One of the other angels points out that rather than be in a lower state than he thinks he deserves, Satan would prefer not to be at all.

It's also interesting to note that Satan can never be sincerely satanic; he realizes, somehow, the foundations of his own being: the futility of sin. At the deepest level, Satan represents the unavoidability of truth. He frequently breaks down in the poem, and he's continually paranoid that, in fact, everything is still God's plan—his fall, the temptation of Adam and Eve, and their eventual redemption. Of course, Satan's paranoia turns out to be right. The tree, which Satan believed was his bait for Adam and Eve, turns out to be God's bait for Satan; God uses Satan's temptation to pave the way for Christ's redemption and elevation of humanity.

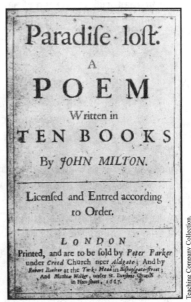

Milton's best known work, *Paradise Lost,* is an epic poem deeply learned in Calvinist and Puritan theology.

Although they are perfected humans, Adam and Eve are innocent of sin, and that innocence complicates their relationship to the events that unfold within and around them. They are warned about sin by the angel Rafael, but they don't quite understand what it is they are being warned about; thus, the warning is not particularly useful. Eve's sin is more a matter of careless folly, vanity, and pride than of deliberate, satanic evil. Adam's decision to eat the apple after Eve has done so is both a sign of his love for her and of the misordering of his loves. If he had properly loved God, he would have rejected Eve. The fact that Adam takes full responsibility before God reveals the difference between satanic and human sin: Satanic sin is often just about itself; human sin often ropes in others.

The Fall does not defeat God's plan. As Satan suspected, God foreknows the Fall and foreknows its certainty of happening, but God does not preordain it. The difference between God knowing that something will happen and commanding that thing to happen is God's participation in time from the perspective of eternity. From any perspective within time, God's knowledge of future events will look like foreknowledge. But from God's eternal presence to all moments of time, everything has already happened, so God knows everything before history even begins. God also knows that God will use the Fall to create an even greater story: that of Christ and redemption.

Many have wondered whether Milton's representation of Satan is too powerful. Satan's psychic agony and his paranoia about God conspire to present a remarkably seductive picture of evil: vivid, vigorous, terrifically driven. In contrast, God, Christ, the good angels, and even Adam and Eve seem pale and tepid. But Milton's depiction of evil in its purest satanic form is not an elevation of Satan. When we consider the motives and rationales of Satan and Adam, if there is any tragedy in the poem, it lies in Adam's choice of Eve, not in Satan's choice of himself. ∎

Name to Know

Milton, John (1608–1674 C.E.). Born in London and received an elite education with help from his wealthy father. Milton enrolled at Christ's College, Cambridge, where he received his M.A. but continued his learning far beyond his university education.

Important Term

Paradise Lost: Epic poem composed by John Milton, an English poet in the 17th century.

Suggested Reading

Beer, *Milton: Poet, Pamphleteer, and Patriot.*

Milton, *Paradise Lost*, Teskey, ed.

1. Is Milton's Satan too intriguing, or does Milton's sympathetic portrait instead offer us a nice meditation on the intelligibility and seductiveness of evil?

2. How should we understand Satan's worry over divine providence in Milton's poem? Could Satan's fall, and the origin of evil itself, in fact be part of God's plan all along?

The Enlightenment and Its Discontents
Lecture 19

Leibniz thinks God has chosen to create a world with free beings who were able to sin and probably would sin, because freedom, even if it was infected and defected by sin—made defective—is still a better thing considered on its own than if we had no freedom in the world at all.

The 17th-century Enlightenment suggested that humans should now, in our full maturity, attempt to address by reason what we had earlier taken on faith and accepted with resignation, namely, that evil could be comprehended and would eventually be conquered. In this lecture, we'll look at three crucial moments in this challenge: the debate between Pierre Bayle and Gottfried Leibniz, the debate between Voltaire and Rousseau, and the amalgamation of these debates in the thinking of David Hume.

Our first debate, that between Bayle and Leibniz, focuses on the question of the proper ambition of the human intellect. Bayle was a fideist, someone who is skeptical about reason's powers to determine most things. He believed that people's deepest convictions are effectively immune from rational assessment and that debate and philosophical analysis are particularly pointless when it comes to religious belief, because people's choices are simply too idiosyncratic in this arena. He famously wrote, "Evil is a problem that reduces all philosophy to hopelessness." Bayle also argued that Manicheanism—the view that proclaimed a metaphysical dualism of rival substances of good and evil in the basic fabric of the cosmos—was the most straightforward philosophical account of evil, considered without appeal to Christian revelation.

Leibniz possessed the most acute philosophical mind of his age. His most famous work, the *Theodicy*, is an extended defense of abstract philosophizing about evil that does not presume any of the assumptions of the Christian faith. Here, Leibniz asserts that the world we inhabit can be proved to be the work of a just and perfectly good God who creates only the best. God is constrained by nothing but logical possibility. Before God begins creating, God intends pure good in its simplest form; then, once creation is underway,

God does the best that can be done with the matter at hand, within the constraints of logic. Thus, we live in "the best of all possible worlds"; it has, Leibniz thinks, the minimal possible evil for the maximal possible good.

Almost a century later, in the wake of the devastating Lisbon earthquake, Voltaire and Rousseau carried on a second version of the Leibniz/Bayle debate. The earthquake stood as the epitome of the problem of natural evil and prompted philosophers to try to make sense of it. Voltaire criticized the optimistic theodicies of Leibniz and others from the basis of the reality of the earthquake. He argued that justifications of these sorts of events are inevitably useless, distracting us from our practical obligations with theoretical questions. For Voltaire, to ask theoretical questions when confronted with practical evil is a profound misconstrual of our own moral and intellectual obligations. Voltaire's hostility to theodicy seems to emerge from his overall skepticism about intellectual efforts; they are simply not grounded in reality.

> **[Rousseau] further suggests that optimism itself—the tendency humans have to look for signs of hope—is a philosophically significant fact about the human condition.**

Rousseau believed that Voltaire's critique of optimistic theodicies was anti-intellectual and cruel. Evil presents us with important concerns on both a practical and an intellectual level. Even if we don't like some formulation of the intellectual effort to address these concerns, to simply turn off our brains is an anti-human thing to do. He further suggests that optimism itself—the tendency humans have to look for signs of hope—is a philosophically significant fact about the human condition. Humans are hopeful, intelligent, meaning-seeking creatures; our optimism suggests that in the face of evil, we can well rely on a kind of supra-rational hope as a mode of response. The source of evil is the same energies that are the wellspring of human hope; evil stems from the misuse of free will and the misappropriation of our optimism.

Hume offers a kind of synthesis of these various views. He believes that theory can lead us in unpleasant directions, writing: "Is [God] willing to prevent evil, but not able? Then is he impotent. Is [God] able, but not willing? Then is he malevolent." But Hume thinks the real problem is that theory gets us nowhere in understanding the place of evil in rational religion; the world is simply too open to offer much in the way of clarity about religious beliefs. Nonetheless, humans do want order to exist, and we do want to care for one another. We are naturally moral and hopeful. Evil and suffering exist, but so do goodness and decency. These facts leave us with a kind of bemused uncertainty about how to formulate theoretical beliefs. But for Hume, this is not a bad thing; we ought to be less concerned with abstract beliefs and more with helping those in need and living our lives to the fullest. ■

Suggested Reading

Antognazza, *Leibniz: An Intellectual Biography*.

Hume, *Dialogues Concerning Natural Religion*.

Leibniz, *Theodicy: Essays on the Goodness of God, the Freedom of Man, and the Origin of Evil*, Huggard, trans.

Neiman, *Evil in Modern Thought: An Alternative History of Philosophy*.

Questions to Consider

1. The Enlightenment thinkers returned in a powerfully new way to the connection between evil and ignorance, this time with an optimistic twist. Is evil merely a name for good that has not yet been understood?

2. What do you think of Voltaire's insistence that justifications and theorizing about evil are useless distractions? Does philosophical reflection on evil do any good at all?

3. Is the case for Manicheanism as compelling as the thinking of such Enlightenment figures as Hume and Bayle? Is the belief in an equally strong power opposing God the most plausible explanation for the existence of evil?

Kant—Evil at the Root of Human Agency
Lecture 20

> Throughout his mature work, Kant tried to show that human reason has real power but also real limit and that the best exercise of that reason is to use it to chart the limits of human thinking and, thereby, to deduce as clearly as possible without direct knowledge what it cannot properly know.

Immanuel Kant is, simply, the most revolutionary and foundational thinker of the modern world. Yet for all his intellectual power, he led quite a pedestrian life. He was born, lived, and worked his entire life in the town of Königsberg in East Prussia. With the publication of the massive *Critique of Pure Reason*, he effectively accomplished a Copernican revolution in philosophy, shifting the focus of philosophical attention from objects—the outside world—to the subject—the human being and the puzzle of how we can know our world.

© 2011 Clipart.com, a division of Getty Images.

Immanuel Kant (1724–1804) shifted the focus of philosophical attention from objects to the subject, to the knowing and acting subject.

In the *Critique of Pure Reason*, Kant suggested that metaphysical theodicies, such as that offered by Leibniz, cannot accomplish what they set out to prove. Like Hume, Kant thought that the evidence of the world was simply indeterminate on the question of the goodness of God. Furthermore, that indeterminacy extends so far as to make any explicitly theoretical claims in this realm of thinking finally not confident enough to be defended. Kant believed that something more is required of us than sheer speculative cognition if we are to find a satisfactory response to the problem of evil, and that something was what he called practical reason. Given that theory can't help us intellectually solve the problem of evil, what we need to do is investigate why evil is a problem for us at all. When we undertake this investigation, we discover that we have another source of quasi-knowledge inside us, apart from reason, in the persistent urging of our will toward resisting evil and working to repair it where we can. In short, it is our will that tells us what is evil and makes us experience it as evil. This experience of the will's opposition to evil is the basis of what Kant calls practical reason properly understood.

For our study, Kant's most important work is *Religion within the Limits of Bare Reason*. It is an exploration of "rational religion," which is all we can know about religion from the perspective of human reason. This is an assessment of the core rational principles on which any religion must be founded, stripped of the historical trappings imposed by particular faiths.

Kant's language of radical evil means to be a sober acknowledgment of the profundity of human corruption, while also insisting that humans have brought this condition on themselves.

Kant insisted that Christian dogmas of original sin get at the universal truth that **radical evil** operates at the base of the human will. Kant locates radical evil in a fundamental disposition of the will to privilege itself over the general good. It is a corruption of our core "moral maxim," prompting us to act out of a "maxim of sensible self-interest"; we treat others as instruments in a drama that is all about our own self-glorification. But this corruption can never be total; we must admit that other people exist, and we know that on some level, they matter beyond our own self-interest. That means that evil is always partial and always builds on a kind of irrationality. Nonetheless, for Kant, this corruption of our moral maxim is so deep that it requires a radical transformation of our overall character, an awakening to the reality that there are other people in the world who have as much moral import as we do.

To many of his readers, Kant's views on radical evil seemed to return to the old superstitions that intellectuals had fought so hard to escape. But for Kant, the language of radical evil was meant to capture the truth latent in traditional religious understandings, namely, that evil's elimination from our lives is not easy or straightforward and is not entirely describable in terms of rational, self-willed human action. His language of radical evil means to be a sober acknowledgment of the profundity of human corruption, while also insisting that humans have brought this condition on themselves.

Kant pioneered a method known as "demythologizing," in which the resolution to a problem we face is recognized to go beyond mere cognition to an appreciation of the power and wisdom of myth; nevertheless, this myth still admits itself to some kind of analysis. The demythologizer is suspicious of the idea that an individual, simply thinking through problems alone, will come to suitable answers. Myth (religion) has a profundity of meaning and a density of symbolic reference beyond the ability of any philosophical system to fully articulate. With this approach, Kant gave us an intellectual style of thinking about evil that has grown increasingly popular over the centuries, that is, not simply to dismiss the past as irrelevant but to appreciate it and, at the same time, to handle it with gloves made entirely of reason. ∎

Name to Know

Kant, Immanuel (1724–1804 C.E.). Born in Königsberg, Prussia, where he lived all his life. A student at the University of Königsberg, Kant made several important contributions to astronomy in his early career before turning increasingly to philosophy.

Important Term

radical evil: The term used by Immanuel Kant to describe the fundamental disposition of the will to privilege itself over the general good.

Suggested Reading

Kant, *Religion within the Boundaries of Mere Reason and Other Writings*, Wood and di Giovanni, trans.

Questions to Consider

1. Does Kant's concept of radical evil accurately reflect what earlier Christians meant by original sin?

2. Do all human beings actually possess a fundamental disposition of the will to privilege itself over the general good?

3. Was Kant correct to argue (against previous Enlightenment thinkers) that the problem of evil cannot finally be answered by theoretical reason alone?

Hegel—The Slaughter Block of History
Lecture 21

> The U.S. Civil War, for example, is itself not just a dumb event; it is, in a complicated way, an intellectual event. It is an attempt in part by the two sides, the two bodies of competence, to understand the meaning of the American Revolution, as people on both sides of that war recognized. The Civil War was an intellectual struggle as much as it was a military struggle.

In this lecture, we'll look at two aspects of the work of Georg Wilhelm Friedrich Hegel: first, his construal of the meaning of original sin and the nature of evil for humans and, second, his assessment of the overall place of evil and the role it plays in history.

The Enlightenment rejected the doctrine of original sin as primitive and unscientific, but Hegel saw it as a consequence of human reflexivity, the ability of humans to step back and think about themselves as they are doing something. Thinking naturally estranges us from our immediate situation; we become self-conscious, which is a form of sin for Hegel. To render ourselves as available as objects of thought is, in some sense, to lose our original organic integrity.

Further, Hegel sees that humanity is clearly at odds with the world and its true nature. The doctrine of original sin, in any of the various religious formulas it's offered, may be stale or mythological, but the insight being communicated is profound: We do, in fact, exist in a state of inevitable and seemingly inescapable estrangement from the world and ourselves. The Fall is the rupture of pure unself-conscious identity into a split awareness. That's formulated as evil, but it brings with it an awareness of the lost status as one that was good. Sin is not only an experience we experience in itself, but it also gives us a kind of nostalgia for an endemic earlier state. Hegel thinks this condition is necessary for our maturation into complete self-consciousness, which somehow entails a return to a complete absorption in the context in which we find ourselves, something like a master musician performing his or her craft.

For Hegel, the story of history is, on one level, about the human intellect coming into maturity through its reflection on history and its struggle to understand the story of its own development. This picture assumes that history actually means something that we can understand and render intelligible to ourselves. History is an activity or a process, but it is in part a process driven forward by people attempting to discern just what that process means. The very activity of questioning shapes the events that come afterwards.

For Hegel, reality is essentially rational, and the core of history is an intelligible story of how both the human and the "World Spirit" are coming to know themselves.

It's true that we attempt to make history intelligible all the time, but Hegel extends this claim audaciously: History is not only the human mind coming to understand itself, but in fact, the mind is involved in a much larger working out of something far more vast than merely the human, namely, God's unfolding self-understanding. For Hegel, reality is essentially rational, and the core of history is an intelligible story of how both the human and the "World Spirit" are coming to know themselves. Having chosen, over many thousands of years, this course of history—however filled with evil and mysterious suffering it may be—the World Spirit chooses this history as the story of its own realization of its power. This representation of God means that God is using the whole of history—and human attempts to understand history—to make sense of God. We are, thus, bit players in a history far greater than we can currently comprehend.

In Hegel's view, then, history has a certain telling that makes sense, and that telling is, in some sense, a rational telling. Consider the phenomenon of the Black Death. It killed about half of Europe, but it also created the conditions for the Reformation. A thing that can devastate a civilization at one moment may, in fact, turn out to enable that civilization to survive and prosper in other ways in the future. This is what Hegel calls the "cunning of reason." Still, we can't always, at the moment, tell just what reason is meaning to do; all we know is that, in the end, it will make sense. Thus, history can be said to be providentially governed, and the true philosophy of history is a theodicy, a justification of all the suffering that has happened.

Hegel's theodicy is not, however, the mechanical and static kind that Leibniz offered. Hegel has a more organic and developmental understanding of evil. He begins with the idea of divine providence, but once he adopts a view of God as immanent in human history, the only conclusion left is that events that are real are justified precisely because they are necessary. The Lisbon earthquake, devastating as it was, was a necessary part of the World Spirit's coming to know itself. Further, Hegel doesn't attempt to reconcile humans to the existence of evil. In his view, concrete evils happen as part of the unfolding of the logic of history, but they are ultimately justified by the course of history, and in that justification, they turn out never to have been evils at all. ■

Name to Know

Hegel, G. W. F. (1770–1831 C.E.). Born in Stuttgart, Germany. When he was 13, his mother died of fever, which Hegel and his father both caught and barely survived. After completing his early education, Hegel enrolled at the seminary in Tübingen, where he became friends with Friedrich Schelling, later a well-known philosopher.

Suggested Reading

Hegel, *Phenomenology of Spirit*, Miller, trans.

Pinkard, *Hegel: A Biography*.

Questions to Consider

1. What do you think of Hegel's view of original sin? Can it be that the fact of human thinking itself is the origin of sin and evil? What do you think of Hegel's claim that "human beings are not what they ought to be"?

2. Does history truly have a meaning and spirit behind it, as Hegel claimed? Or, as is often asserted, is history merely one damned thing after another?

3. Can Hegel's account of history take evil seriously enough? If all is necessary, can evil really be anything more than disguised good?

Marx—Materialism and Evil
Lecture 22

> Marx did think it was a pretty shocking thing that some people had all this wealth and they wouldn't share it with other people—but he did think that talking about it as immoral was not as fully powerful a way of talking about it as simply pointing out the bare material facts. He thought that understanding those facts … would be a more powerful motivator for effecting change than preaching to people in any way.

Karl **Marx** came to understand Hegel's work as offering a new philosophical vision for the shape of understanding the world and guiding human action within it. As history moved on, the world was changing, and history was changing precisely because humans were coming to self-conscious awareness of their own power and their own capacities to change the world and themselves. Hegel believed that history is a story about God coming to maturation and self-realization, while for Marx, it is about the self-realization of humanity.

Marx is not a theoretical innovator in thinking about evil; rather, he's an exemplary figure for a practical response to it. He was Hegelian in imagining that the resolution of the problem of evil is one dimension of the goal of human history. But unlike Hegel, Marx's understanding of the human is materialist, meaning that material circumstances, not ideas, determine human thought and action. Further, without the right material conditions, people can't think the thoughts that will revolutionize material conditions. Marx believed that evil is due to social conditions and material inequalities. Against Hegel, he insisted that evil is the result of these inequalities and, therefore, is contingent, not necessary; it would be overcome within history, not at its end.

For Marx, evil is a structure of unequal social relations in which some are able to gather wealth—"capital"—from others' labor and reinvest that wealth in ways that make those inequalities ever greater. Over time, enormous concentrations of wealth occur, and this wealth creates its own rationale for how the world should be run. Material wealth, for Marx, is a social force and a social reality more fundamental than political power.

Material inequalities lead to differences in other realms of human life—in education, in comfort, and in health—and these differences, Marx thought, lead people to either do or not do wicked things. If we lived in a social order of total equality, in which people were given all they needed to cultivate themselves and they gave back to the whole the fruits of their self-cultivation, evil wouldn't exist. For Marx, socialism is about self-cultivation and expression; the joy we have in our action lies in the cultivation and exercise of our talents, not in the products of our talents. This is not what came to be understood as socialism in the Eastern Bloc of communist nations governed by the Soviet Union for most of the second half of the 20th century. Marx wasn't interested in a revolution of the social order; he was interested in a revolution of human expectations and longings. He wanted us to get beyond the idea that we are in the world to acquire goods and come to see ourselves as creatures who find joy in the exercise of the gifts and skills that we have.

Karl Marx (1818–1883) believed that religion was nothing but alienated human longing, but also the most powerful reality in human history.

According to Marx, changes in social conditions and material inequalities can alter or even eliminate the big evils of human life—starvation, war, slavery— because the basic cause of these evils— disparities of wealth—would disappear. Note that Marx is not talking about a philosophical resolution of the problem of evil; he's thinking of a resolution in terms of the practical disappearance of concrete evil itself. But this vision can undergird an ethic of brutal consequentialism: Once you're convinced you know the remedy for suffering and evil, you can justify a great deal in seeking to eliminate them. Morality becomes contingent on decency, and to get to decency, anything may be necessary.

Marx raises two questions for our study, one theoretical and one practical. The theoretical question: Does the approach that Marx offers—an approach that focuses ruthlessly on a practical solution to the problem of evil—offer enough respect to theoretical questions about evil? Part of the problem here lies in Marx's understanding of history: At any moment when there is suffering in the world, we will ultimately understand that suffering to have been justified, because later events caused by the suffering will be much better than they would have been absent the suffering. In other words, every moment in history doesn't have its own integrity; its ultimate significance is only part of a larger story. Another view of history believes that each moment in history has a kind of moral sense that is determinant in itself. The moment that evil or good occurs bears its own significance, and here, no matter what the justification of suffering is in the future, the suffering of the moment still demands an answer.

> **Against Hegel, [Marx] insisted that evil is the result of these inequalities and, therefore, is contingent, not necessary; it would be overcome within history, not at its end.**

The practical question raised by Marx's approach is more immediate and direct: Is it viable to say that evil can be solved in the way Marx suggests? The history of Marxism after Marx certainly does not give us confidence that Marxism became a device for ameliorating human suffering. ∎

Name to Know

Marx, Karl (1818–1883 C.E.). Born and educated in Trier, Germany. He enrolled at the University of Bonn but later transferred to the University of Berlin. There, Marx encountered the Young Hegelians, a group of thinkers who advocated for radical political proposals in conversation with Hegelian philosophy.

Suggested Reading

Marx and Engels, *The Marx-Engels Reader*, Tucker, ed.

Questions to Consider

1. In Karl Marx, we see a strongly practical approach to the problem of evil and an insistence that evil is fundamentally a problem of material conditions. Is Marx convincing in his claim that changes in social conditions can finally eradicate evil?

2. In what ways does Marx's account of evil appear more optimistic than Hegel's? In what ways does it seem less optimistic?

3. Will theoretical explanations of evil always be desired, or are they merely a symptom of material inequalities?

The American North and South—Holy War
Lecture 23

> It's a very acute psychology of how a society's vision of right and wrong
> can go horrendously awry, and in certain ways, it prophesies forward
> to what happens in the 20th century with various kinds of genocides;
> especially, as we'll see, the work of Hannah Arendt resonates with
> Twain quite powerfully on the Holocaust.

The Civil War represented a theological crisis for America, a struggle between two opposite understandings of Scripture and what God meant for the world. The central conflict, of course, was the presence of slavery in American life. In this lecture, we'll look at how two thinkers, Mark Twain and Abraham Lincoln, explored the relationship between slavery and Americans' conception of their mission in the world.

The Adventures of Huckleberry Finn is Twain's brilliant, clearly sincere protest against the kind of moral corruption that Huck both represents and is victimized by, a moral corruption that infected the whole of his society. This corruption is revealed in Huck's belief that he has committed a crime in helping his friend Jim to escape from slavery. Jim's owner, Miss Watson, has tried to make Huck a good person, but Huck believes himself to be utterly immoral—and destined for hell—because he can't obey the law and turn in Jim. Twain is telling us that the upstanding Victorian morality Huck has tried to adopt is actually a horrific, hypocritical hostility to human beings.

The conclusion here is that we ought not to let "morality"—our beliefs about what's right and wrong—float too free from ordinary human empathy. The conscience should be fed, Twain implies, both by rigorous and skeptical argument and by concrete attention to realities brought to awareness by our vital human affections. The danger is in not seeing that any one version of morality may need to be changed; if it is not changed, we may end up, like Huck, jettisoning our concern about morality altogether.

Although Twain didn't offer much of a solution to the problem he so devastatingly diagnosed, Abraham Lincoln's Second Inaugural Address serves as a hypothetical roadmap for where Lincoln would have liked the nation to go. In this speech, Lincoln frames the Civil War as God's judgment on the people of the United States, both North and South, for their collective complicity in the sin of slavery. He transforms what would have been, for many of his contemporaries, a dualism of good and evil—the South on one side, the North on the other—into two sides of a community, both of which have sinned grievously in God's eyes; now, God chooses to punish them and, thus, expiate their sins.

At this point in his political leadership, Lincoln was pivoting away from a focus on fighting the war to healing the nation, and it's interesting that he does so from a theological standpoint. Both sides of the war understood themselves to be fighting for God's cause. Lincoln suggests that we can understand the moral energies of both sides, but we must redirect them. We must recognize that both sides are fighting as penitents in a war that works out their own complicity in sin and let God decide the outcome of that war as a way of resolving that sin. Lincoln's speech is astonishing for a number of reasons: its theological register from a person who wasn't, apparently, very theological; its mercy from a leader on the verge of defeating his enemies; and its invitation for both sides to reconsider the war not as a just war against evil but as a history of just punishment that all ought to accept and reply to with humility.

> **Lincoln viewed [the evil of slavery] as one that both North and South had collaborated in producing and profited from; now, both needed to confront their complicity in this evil.**

Lincoln saw the evil that lay at the core of the war itself: the vast and dehumanizing system of slavery. But he also viewed this evil as one that both North and South had collaborated in producing and profited from; now, both needed to confront their complicity in this evil. In this, Lincoln offers a vision of how to think about evil and how to think about our own involvement in evil that might be of use beyond his own context. In suggesting that humans should defuse their tendencies toward dualism in moral conflicts, Lincoln invites us to view our enemies as fellow humans involved in a larger mutual project.

Both Twain and Lincoln were prophets well ahead of their time. Twain seems to predict the way a society can misshape its adherence to morals in ways that scholars of the Holocaust would later parallel. Twain's appreciation of how morality can conspire to reinforce racism is also at the heart of Martin Luther King's insistence that the civil rights movement was as much a struggle for white people as for black people. And Lincoln's insistence that we are all complicit and should recognize our complicity is a reminder that Americans are always one people, for good and ill, united both in our aspirations and our crimes. Further, if we can find ways of overcoming the mythology of dualism, we may find ourselves better able to live into the future. ■

Suggested Reading

Noll, *America's God: Jonathan Edwards to Abraham Lincoln*.

Twain, *The Adventures of Huckleberry Finn*, Cooley, ed.

Questions to Consider

1. Reflecting on Twain's *Huckleberry Finn*, do you think that morality can sometimes be the bearer of evil rather than evil's enemy? How can we know whether our morality may be corrupt?

2. If Lincoln were alive today, what observations might he make about America's current political, cultural, and even military conflicts? Could Lincoln's arguments in the Second Inaugural for God's providence and "malice toward none, charity for all" offer any consolation to us, or is Lincoln's time too different from our own?

Nietzsche—Considering the Language of Evil
Lecture 24

Nietzsche is hard to figure out. I don't think I understand him yet; it's not clear to me that I ever will understand him. In fact, I'm not even sure that he wanted to be understood in the sense of having his thought be perfectly transparent to another intellect. I think he wanted more to provoke and inspire, to agitate and excite, not to offer something that could ever be fully cognitively digested.

Friedrich Nietzsche's most famous claim is that "God is dead," killed by us. And once we have killed God, we have to think about how to live beyond that belief, that is, beyond the language of good and evil.

For our purposes, Nietzsche's main argument is that morality is not only incorrect, but it no longer serves any useful purpose in our world. The concepts of good and evil that we think of as naturally part of the world are not, in fact, applicable to the world as we find it. The language of good and evil, the language of truth, the assumption that we need to inquire into truth—these are all tools of our own devising that have outlived their usefulness for us. They have served a purpose in convincing us that the world is organized by these categories, but Nietzsche thinks now that the world is not.

For Nietzsche, the human is an animal that uses language and thought to make its way in the world, but the language we've developed has trapped us in an unhealthy position. Much of our ethical thinking is linguistically shaped and, in some

Teaching Company Collection.

In *Beyond Good and Evil*, Friedrich Nietzsche (1844–1900) argues that morality is something we need to get past because it restricts our will.

ways, linguistically created. But Nietzsche says that in using language, we're always vulnerable to forgetting that the words we use are our words, and we're always tempted to impute to them a metaphysical credibility that they in no way possess.

Nietzsche further argues that the language of good and evil derives from the attempts of some humans to suppress the enthusiastic energies of others. This is the idea of slave morality, that is, the condition in which the weak in human history—the less noble—have the ability to convince the strong—the truly noble spirits of the world—that they should obey the rules the weak live by. In other words, the language of good and evil manages to keep humans ordered in a certain way, and it does so by making the central moral issue for ethics guilt and the avoidance of guilt.

Nature is an energy that seeks ever-new forms of expression; the human is a vessel for that energy, a structure that also seeks ever-new forms of expression.

Nietzsche thus proposes that the language of evil be replaced with a different language, one less freighted with heavy theological connotations. He sees the need for an evaluative framework to assess the fruitfulness of our actions, but he prefers a language for this assessment that is more authentically grounded. One powerful way of organizing that language would be around the concept of health. Here, we would assess actions by asking to what extent they are "life-promoting, life-preserving … even species-cultivating." The real problem with the dichotomy of good and evil is that it serves to keep humans stuck in patterns of behavior and constrains the development and exercise of our intellectual and physical powers.

Nietzsche also wants us to challenge what he calls the "will to truth," our unstated, almost-reflexive assumption that seeking truth as an objective reality outside of us is innately good—that if our thoughts do not generate some kind of evidence from the outside that they might be true, then they are probably false. Nietzsche argues that we need to turn the will to truth on itself and inquire into whether it is healthy for us. When we do that, we'll see that it assumes the world is composed of structures of opposites, but no such tidy oppositions exist in nature.

Nature, for Nietzsche, is a struggle, an overcoming of the moment for something greater than the moment. The human is the creature whose nature is not yet fully known and whose nature is open to the human to determine. Nature is an energy that seeks ever-new forms of expression; the human is a vessel for that energy, a structure that also seeks ever-new forms of expression. This means that the forms we have at any moment are always going to be broken apart in a new expression of the energy that is coming. This conception of nature is what Nietzsche famously called the "will to power."

Is the will to power something we're in charge of? Are we the ones discharging this will, or are we what is discharged? The psychology that Nietzsche offers understands the will to power as a fundamental force, moving through the world and challenging us, challenging our conception of ourselves as people who are in charge of us. The will to power requires us to take a radical new stance toward ourselves, with new ideas about the soul—the soul as a multiplicity of creatures, the soul as segmented in complicated ways. We will understand this new soul as not good or evil but healthy or sick. This is nothing less than a revolution in our psychologies—in how we think of ourselves and how we will live into the future. ∎

Name to Know

Nietzsche, Friedrich (1844–1900 C.E.). Born and raised in Röcken, a small town near Leipzig, the son of a Lutheran minister who died when he was 5. Nietzsche enrolled at the University of Bonn to study theology but turned to philology after losing his faith.

Nehamas, *Nietzsche: Life as Literature.*

Nietzsche, *Beyond Good and Evil*, Kaufmann, trans.

Nietzsche, *On the Genealogy of Morality: A Polemic*, Clark and Swensen, trans.

Questions to Consider

1. Nietzsche suggested that a moral revolution was necessary—one in which the language of "evil" ought to be discarded altogether. Does the language of evil serve an indispensable purpose, or would we do well to follow Nietzsche in discarding it altogether?

2. Is morality reducible to a struggle for power, as Nietzsche argued? Is any moral system always designed to empower some and suppress others?

3. Should we take Nietzsche's advice and turn our attention away from truth and toward health?

Dostoevsky—The Demonic in Modernity
Lecture 25

Dostoevsky thinks the very genre of the novel itself is a product of Western secularity. The novel, as an imaginary story, an imaginary creation by a human author of a kind of vivid human world—Dostoevsky finds that enormously theologically problematic. It's potentially latently a rival to God's creation—any novel is—and so, potentially, a novel is intrinsically corruptive.

In this lecture, we turn to perhaps the greatest philosophical novelist of all time, **Fyodor Dostoevsky**. Dostoevsky's works repeatedly struggle with what happens to humans when they operate outside of the restraining realities of vivid and organic religious belief in conditions of a rapidly modernizing society.

Throughout his working life, Dostoevsky was obsessed with the challenge of intellectual currents coming from the West, especially with those intellectual movements that attacked traditional morality and religion. He saw the new ideas of his time as powerfully revolutionary, but unlike Nietzsche, who thought such ideas were good and exciting, Dostoevsky felt that they were nightmares that would lead to a new age of barbarism and inhumanity.

As we've seen, nihilism is the belief that there is no moral structure, no absolute framework to the cosmos. The cosmos is what we make of it. Dostoevsky found nihilism a seductive idea, but he also thought that it ultimately doesn't work with the psychology of humans. The terror for Dostoevsky is that this belief has deleterious effects on people who hold it and those around them.

In *Demons*, Dostoevsky argues that the desire of revolutionary modernists in Russia and elsewhere to improve society founders as a result of their failure to understand the nature of evil. The novelist makes use of the tradition of a multiplicity of devils in Eastern Orthodox Christianity to identify and describe the anarchic squabbling nature of evil, particularly as it is manifest in groups of revolutionaries. The problem with rebels is that we can't take them seriously from a practical standpoint, but their actions can have deadly consequences. Here, Dostoevsky is sketching a distinctly modern character: the figure of the human whose impact on reality is out of all proportion to his or her own pathetic, ludicrous reality. A tension exists between the smallness of this figure and the magnitude of the evil that he or she is able to produce.

The story of *Demons* revolves around a group of young revolutionaries and the murder of a former member of the group, Ivan Shatov. Shatov's break with the group can be traced to his more morally supple and vivid picture of reality than that seen by the revolutionaries, one in which morality matters and humans are mired in sin. The revolutionaries, caught up in the currents of 19th-century science, rationalism, and philosophical extremism, have the view that things happen, but responsibility can't be pinned on anybody. They are creating

Fyodor Dostoevsky (1821–1881) was obsessed with the challenge of the Western intellectual movements, especially those that attacked traditional morality and religion.

a new world that is superior to the present one; thus, the consequences of their actions will be justified by the endpoint they achieve. In contrast, Shatov tells one of the other group members, "We are all to blame." The distinction between these two attitudes—"we are all to blame" and "no one is to blame"—is, for Dostoevsky, the driving force behind the history of the 19th century.

In *Demons*, Dostoevsky offers us a powerful account of the nature of evil in modernity that is couched primarily in political terms. He sees evil as a revolution against both the social order and the conditions of human existence in general. Further, the modern world doesn't want to acknowledge the reality of this evil. As a response to this corruption, Dostoevsky proposes the tradition of radical orthodoxy, with special focus on the drama of sin and redemption.

Where *Demons* was essentially about a collectivity of people and their collective descent into hell, *Crime and Punishment* focuses on one person: Raskolnikov, a failed graduate student who kills a pawnbroker and her sister. What's interesting to us about this book is the representation of Raskolnikov's motives. He seems to have committed the crime because it would allow him to demonstrate to himself that he is invulnerable to moral guilt or self-condemnation. Of course, in this, Raskolnikov turns out to be wrong. He is traumatized by the events and must finally confess his crimes. He believed his story was that of a liberal Western nihilist, but as Dostoevsky points out, he failed to live into that story. Dostoevsky suggests that the problem with Raskolnikov is that he's trying to usurp God's role, trying to tell his own story instead of living the story that God gives him.

For Dostoevsky, the problem of evil lies in any act of rebellion against an established order. Acquiescence to a powerful authority above us is merely one way that we observe the place in society that God has given us. ■

Name to Know

Dostoevsky, Fyodor (1821–1881 C.E.). The son of a violent alcoholic, a former military surgeon who practiced at a hospital for the poor in Moscow.

Suggested Reading

Dostoevsky, *Crime and Punishment*, Pevear and Volkhonsky, trans.

———, *Demons*, Pevear and Volkhonsky, trans.

Frank, *Dostoevsky: A Writer in His Time*.

Questions to Consider

1. Dostoevsky's *Demons* suggests that modernity's denial of the existence of evil may, in fact, be an even more profound complicity with evil itself. Do we risk a complicity with evil by denying its existence or refusing to consider its effects?

2. What is the place of thinking about evil in the modern world? Has evil become passé, or does it still hold a prominent place in the modern imagination?

Conrad—Incomprehensible Terror

Lecture 26

Conrad really has a quite radically secular vision of evil. People just seem to fall into evil, or be lured into it, for reasons that are in some ways present to themselves; they're reasons that are not demonic or theological, but they are, in some sense, all too human.

This lecture looks at **Joseph Conrad's** vision of the fate of those who have experienced evil in the modern world. For Conrad, those who have seen the traumas of modern war and other forms of suffering may be so estranged from everyday experience that the wisdom they have acquired is incommunicable to those who might learn something from it.

In *Heart of Darkness*, Conrad asks two basic questions: first, whether the modern mind has the capacity to confront evil and, second, whether the mind can communicate the experience of evil to others. The plot of this novella is simple: It's the story of Charlie Marlow, sitting with some friends on a yacht in the Thames, attempting—and failing—to tell the story of another boat trip, one in central Africa. Marlow's experience seems completely unconnected from the experience of the men he is speaking to in the present. Conrad's vision of the "heart of darkness" is not a place where there are uncivilized, primitive people but a place where people are able to be uncivilized in a far more brutal way than those who are supposedly primitive. Marlow encounters the heart of darkness in the unintelligible figure of Kurtz. In fact, the central problem of the novel is precisely Marlow's attempt to understand Kurtz. It's important to note that Kurtz's famous line in the book, "The horror, the horror," is understood neither by those who hear it in the story nor those of us who read it.

On his return trip, Marlow reflects on his encounter with Kurtz. He believes that the phrase uttered by Kurtz must mean something, but he doesn't know what it is. Kurtz, he says, "had stepped over the edge, while I had been permitted to draw back my hesitating foot." Perhaps, Marlow thinks, this is the difference between them: "perhaps all the wisdom, and all truth, and all sincerity, are just compressed into that inappreciable moment of time in which we step over the threshold of the invisible." Kurtz, Marlow believes, possesses a terrible sincerity and vision, while his own vision is clouded.

At the end of the story, Marlow confesses that he didn't tell Kurtz's fiancée the words Kurtz spoke as he lay dying on the boat in the jungle. Although Marlow views this as a failure, Conrad makes it possible for us to judge differently: Perhaps Marlow told the truth, but the fiancée could not properly understand it. Throughout the novel, Marlow is suspicious of words, finding them untrustworthy in their ability to tell the truth. But he also knows that we need words in order to properly see our world. Marlow comes to see that his attempt to tell the story is vexed by his own incapacity to speak it and his audience's incapacity to hear it. Though "the horror" is the most famous line that Conrad ever wrote, there's no way to understand it, no way to know the horror. We are so distanced from the sources of Kurtz's experience that we cannot comprehend his cry.

Joseph Conrad (1857–1924) has a radically secular vision of evil: People just seem to fall into evil, or be lured into it.

Library of Congress, Prints and Photographs Division.

As readers, we want there to be a clear distinction between good and evil in the story. We want Kurtz to have gone wrong and kicked away the constraints of human nature. But one reason Conrad's work is so powerful is that it challenges our belief in that easy distinction. Conrad suggests that Kurtz is beyond good and evil; he may have seen more deeply than the rest of us the reality of our world. At the conclusion of the novel, Conrad also forces us to ask a question about what Marlow tells Kurtz's fiancée. He says that the last word Kurtz spoke was her name, but what if her name is, in fact, "the horror"? Is Conrad making a statement to all of us in civilization? Is the brutality that exists at the edge of civilization actually no more brutal than that which lies at its center?

The question of the apprehensibility of evil framed by *Heart of Darkness* is carried further by Conrad's later novel *The Secret Agent*. Here, we move from evil encountered at the edge of apparent civilization to evil at the very heart of civilization—in London. Conrad forces us to wonder whether the terrorist Verloc's desire to destroy civilization as something wrong and sterile does not exist as a cancer within civilization. Perhaps the idea of civilization itself needs to be rethought; perhaps it gives us only a more subtle version of cruelty and evil. The lesson Conrad tries to teach us seems to be this: We may be able to shunt our darkness off to some faraway corner of the world for the moment, but it remains our darkness, and when we finally encounter it, we will see that it has been with us, unacknowledged, all along. ∎

Name to Know

Conrad, Joseph (1857–1924 C.E.). Born to a noble Polish family under the name of Józef Teodor Konrad Korzeniowsk. Conrad was orphaned at the age of 11, after his mother and father died of sickness.

Suggested Reading

Conrad, *Heart of Darkness*, Armstrong, ed.

Conrad, *The Secret Agent: A Simple Tale*.

Meyers, *Joseph Conrad: A Biography*.

Questions to Consider

1. Is there something incommunicable about experiences of evil, as Conrad seems to imply? Does our experience in modern civilization make us dangerously incapable of recognizing or describing evil?

2. Was Conrad right to subtly suggest that advanced civilization, despite our technological and scientific sophistication, remains incapable of escaping the "heart of darkness"?

Freud—The Death Drive and the Inexplicable
Lecture 27

Almost all the time, adults cannot expect, for [Freud], to radically change their behavior, because the dispositions that we have are too deeply habituated in us to be really significantly reformable. The best we can typically hope for is to manage our various pathologies.

Sigmund Freud's overall picture of the tensions and complexities that go into the human psyche builds on an assessment of the human and human civilization as the site of a war between rival principles of love and death. We desire love, but we also possess a **death drive**, a force or impulse that seeks annihilation. Freud also sees an ill fit between ourselves as individuals and our role in human culture and society. This tension has inadvertently generated systems of morality that we use to describe and control this ill fit. Freud's overall account is an alternative to other moral accounts, a picture of both our desires for human affiliation and civilization and the various discontents that civilization produces in us.

Freud's most basic tenet was what we call the **pleasure principle**, the idea that people want happiness, yet happiness is something we feel by contrast with normalcy. In response to this problem, humans have tried to moderate the desire for happiness in various ways, but none of these practices works perfectly. Our desire for happiness and satisfaction can be met only to a degree.

Civilization arises from our need for protection and the desire for happiness. It is rooted in social and political necessities, but it also has a more properly physiological basis in our drive toward sexual and supra-sexual union with others. This drive Freud named Eros, the principle of love. Much of psychoanalysis focuses on where this drive goes wrong, seeking to uncover how our desires obstruct our functioning as humans.

Freud notes that love itself creates resentment against civilization, because civilization restricts sexual life precisely as it expands the cultural unit. Monogamy is the price humans pay to become civilized, and that tradeoff generates resentment. As we said, there is a tension between ourselves as humans and our role in human society. This ill fit creates discontents that express themselves in self-destructive behavior or behavior that is destructive of others.

Along with our understandable resentments at the curtailing of our libidos, Freud believed that another mysterious force is at work in us, a force that actively and intentionally seeks our own destruction and that of the world. This death drive brings into the picture the potential of human nature for cruelty. Freud's account of evil, if we think of it in terms of the death drive, is a resistance to accept any form of what he saw as "consolation"—religious, moral, philosophical, romantic, even psychoanalytic—in lieu of the actual reality of the absurd presence of a destructive force in the psyche. In other words, Freud wants to say that by naming the death drive, we are doing the least consoling thing possible; we are identifying a significant problem at the heart of our being that we will never be able to solve.

Monogamy is the price humans pay to become civilized, and that tradeoff generates resentment.

Freud posited the death drive when he realized that "hunger and love" alone are inadequate principles to explain "what moves the world." He decided that there must be another, contrary instinct seeking to break down those units and return them to a more fundamental state of pure potentiality. The destructiveness of the death drive is not only outwardly oriented; in fact, it's rooted in a "silent" instinct that all humans possess. It is always intertwined with the love drive and works only by warping the love drive; it never positively exists on its own.

These two drives—the love and the death drive—meet in the human soul, the psyche. It is the need of civilization to suppress the death drive, leading to its sublimation; this, in turn, results in the heavy burden of guilt felt by all people. The resentments caused by the desire to repress or sublimate the destructive energies each one of us has causes tensions in our souls. The discontents of civilization are rooted, then, in our inability to escape our instinctual aggressiveness. Civilization exacerbates the pressures of the death drive by forcing us also to sublimate the love drive, redirecting that energy into the same pool as aggressive energy.

Ultimately, Freud tells us that civilization is the result of the struggle of these two instincts in humans. He further says, ruthlessly dismissing traditional morality, "And it is this battle of the giants that our nurse-maids try to appease with their lullaby about Heaven." Traditional morality cannot make sense of the struggle between these two powerful natural drivers.

This view is remarkably pessimistic, but there is some hope. Freud suggests that Eros can gain the upper hand on the death drive, if only for a time. Still, Freud saw that in the modern world, humans possess powerful destructive abilities; the death drive has reached the possibility for its own complete consummation. ■

Name to Know

Freud, Sigmund (1856–1939 C.E.). Born in Píbor, a village in the Austro-Hungarian Empire, to poor Jewish parents, who sacrificed to provide their son with an excellent education. The family eventually moved to Vienna, where Freud studied and, later, joined the medical faculty at the University of Vienna.

Important Terms

death drive: Term used by Sigmund Freud to describe the instinct opposite to Eros in the human psyche that seeks to dissolve the world back into a primeval, inorganic state.

pleasure principle: Term coined by Sigmund Freud to describe our desire to be happy and feel pleasure, while acknowledging that happiness is not a normal state of human life.

Freud, *Civilization and Its Discontents*, Strachey, trans.

Lear, *Freud*.

Questions to Consider

1. As noted in this lecture, Freud believed that pleasure played a definitive role in human motivation and served as one of the ultimate justifications of our actions. What is the relationship between the "good" and the "pleasurable"? Is the good always pleasurable? Is the pleasurable always good? Which of these is more fundamental?

2. Are certain human actions really expressions of the desire for destruction, as Freud's concept of the death drive suggests? Is the desire for death a silent desire in human beings?

Camus—The Challenge to Take Evil Seriously
Lecture 28

Does our moral self-understanding—the way we picture the world as a whole, the shape of our lives within it—really help us come to grips with the realities that we call "evil"? This is one of Camus' most profound themes in all his writings. Is it possible, he worries, that there is something in human nature that makes it hard to take evil seriously enough?

People had thought that World War I was a terrible event for humanity, but in comparison, World War II was apocalyptic. Intellectuals believed that after the war, humans would be forced to change dramatically, but normalcy was recovered with astonishing speed. Among the responses to this recovery was that of the brilliant thinker and writer Albert Camus. Two of his books in particular have significance for our study: *The Plague* and *The Fall*.

In *The Plague*, Camus allegorizes the corruption of a society by evil through the metaphor of a plague infesting a city. The novel tracks the responses of the citizens to the various problems brought on by the plague. Of course, the plague here is not just a biological pestilence; it is an allegory for Nazi evil. Camus uses various characters in the novel, including a doctor and a priest, as devices to explore how certain sets of belief will work themselves out in confrontation with absolute evil.

One of the most interesting and thought-provoking themes in the book is the extreme resistance of humanity to coming to terms with, and bringing into focus, the problem of evil itself. Initially, many in the city are reluctant to recognize the plague as something other than an ordinary illness. As the suffering goes on, the citizens seek some cosmic explanation for the plague so that they can "fix" it. Finally, the wisest among the citizens come to realize that their questions about the causes of the plague are unanswerable and may serve as distractions from the reality of evil. The best response is not to worry about the questions but to face the plague and fight it for what it is.

When the plague is finally defeated, one of the characters comments on the astonishing speed with which people in the city return to a state of normalcy. Indeed, the citizens seem to downplay or deny the reality of the plague, perhaps because they can't process it in relation to ordinary life experience. The lesson of the novel is straightforward: Evil is real; it will confront us, and all we can do is decide how we will respond to it. There is no this-worldly solution to evil; humans will face it repeatedly. *The Plague* closes with what seems a prophetic reminder that evil can lie dormant among us for years before resurfacing.

One of the most interesting and thought-provoking themes in the book is the extreme resistance of humanity to coming to terms with, and bringing into focus, the problem of evil itself.

About eight years after *The Plague*, Camus wrote a far more ambiguous novel, *The Fall*. The narrator here, Jean-Baptiste Clamence, is a man caught in the awareness of his own sin and that of the world in a way that he recognizes but cannot quite name and cannot escape. His name translates to "John the Baptist, crying," bringing to mind a prophet, "a voice crying in the wilderness." But he also lives in the center of the ring of canals in Amsterdam, reminding us of Satan in Dante's *Inferno*.

In the novel, Clamence tells the story of his own collapse, but he does so in order to convince his audience that they are also unworthy. His strategy is seduction by narcissism, yet the seduction he employs is an incredibly self-conscious one: He realizes that the narcissism he deploys to seduce people actually governs his own life, even to the degree that his confession of his sins is an attempt to make his audience admire him.

Clamence was once a successful defense lawyer in Paris, but when he fails to come to the aid of a woman who has fallen from a bridge, his life changes dramatically. He realizes that he has hidden from his self-awareness his own selfishness and narcissism. He lives now in Amsterdam and hides in his apartment a panel from a stolen painting, *The Just Judges*. He cannot stand to have the painting on display because he now has an aversion to thinking about justice; he believes that everyone is guilty. The task for humanity is to find a way to live with our guilt, because there is no way to escape it.

At the end of the novel, we learn that Clamence has an incredible longing to be other than what he is. He doesn't want to be a sinner or a moral failure. He wants to risk his life for something greater than himself, but he lost his one chance to do so. There is no grace, no second chance; we are already and always trapped in sin.

Perhaps Camus' greatest lesson is that we have a difficult time seeing evil and recognizing it for what it is. We would rather avoid seeing it, in the world and in ourselves. But if we could see evil for what it actually is—human corruption—perhaps we could confront and resist it. For Camus, just seeing clearly is a moral victory. ■

Suggested Reading

Camus, *The Fall*, O'Brien, trans.

Camus, *The Plague*, Gilbert, trans.

Todd, *Camus: A Life*, Irvy, trans.

Questions to Consider

1. What do you think of Camus' account of evil as a plague? Is evil a permanent (though sometimes dormant) fact of human existence—an enduring condition of human life? And if Camus was right about this, how do we avoid despair and quietism? If evil is permanent, why resist?

2. The character of Jean-Baptiste Clamence suggests that evil may, in fact, lie behind our lives in more ways than we are aware. Was Camus correct in asserting that our task is not to overcome evil but to learn to live with our guilt?

[F]or [Tillich], as with Luther, the experience of evil is something that the devil seduces you into but does not compel you to do. There's a way that being "possessed" here gets at the genuinely *you* character of the evil act—the way that you are the one doing it—while also getting at the experience of this evil as something alien to your true being.

In thinking about evil, Christians face two important questions: First, can Christianity ever really take evil seriously enough? To many secular thinkers, the gospel can seem desperately optimistic, as if it's trying to overcompensate for the challenge of evil. Second, can Christianity take our age's evil seriously enough? In other words, do theologians manage to show how Christianity can grapple with the problems our world faces today?

Paul Tillich was a German Lutheran theologian who became an important philosophical voice in the years after World War I. In his essay on "the demonic," Tillich defines his subject as a perversion of creativity, a way in which the creativity that is the world's basic principle can go wrong. Sin is not sloth, or lassitude, or despair; it's an active energy. And evil is not simply an absence of good, but it has its own positive "givenness." The demonic exists as the most potent form of that givenness of evil as a tension between creative and destructive powers at the base of reality itself.

The demonic appears when the forms of reality are consumed by what Tillich calls the "transcendent depth of reality"; that is, when the forms in which we understand reality reveal themselves to be unable to fully contain the reality that they capture and deliver to us. If we think about all we can see in a beautifully crafted wooden chair, for example—its origin as a tree, the skill of its builder—we see that it is, in some sense, much more than a chair. And in trying to grasp that depth, Tillich says we begin to experience a vertigo about reality. It's this capacity of reality to overwhelm us, to threaten ordinary life, that for Tillich, is evidence of the demonic. It is especially visible in human personality, which can remain recognizably itself yet be "possessed" by a power beyond itself. For Tillich, grace is a healing of this bottomless character that we have discovered in our own existence.

While Tillich is useful for thinking about the positivity of evil, the Swiss Calvinist theologian Karl Barth explores the negativity of evil. Barth described evil and sin as grounded in "the nothing" that God has refused explicitly to create. This nothing is a genuine threat to everything that exists, it undergirds sin, and it is far more frightening than anything we can imagine. The nothing is a possibility that God might have created had God been different than the God we believe and confess God to be. Nonetheless, God allows a few tendrils of nothingness to creep into reality just so that humans know something of what we are not facing.

Barth described evil and sin as grounded in "the nothing" that God has refused explicitly to create.

For Barth, it is part of the mystery of God that evil exists at all. In some ways echoing the Book of Job, Barth believes that evil is related in a complicated way to the providence of God, and because of that, only the providence of God will be evil's final solution. Barth thinks that all of humanity is predestined to bliss and salvation from before the Fall, but he also tries to understand evil as something humans do as part of God's drama of creation. Thus, he emphasizes the profundity of evil within the context of the greater profundity of God's love for the world. Evil is only defeatable by God, and in fact, God uses it to demonstrate God's immeasurable love for humanity.

Reinhold Niebuhr is the most famous theological voice on evil in the 20th century. He offered an interpretation of traditional Christian visions of sin that reformulates the wisdom of that vision in a language suitable for modern people. According to Niebuhr, "sin presupposes itself"; it is intrinsic to the human condition, yet it is clear that humans should not be sinful. Sin is not necessary for humans, Niebuhr thinks, but it is an inevitable consequence of our current created condition. Humans are created as finite yet free, natural yet transcending nature. We recognize our hybrid constitution and are made anxious by it. It is that inevitable anxiety that induces us to indulge in pride—a denial of our createdness, our materiality—or sensuality—an embrace of materiality to the exclusion of the transcendent.

Grace, for Niebuhr, is the energy that allows us to go forward in our lives, knowing that our judgment is to come as sinners but also knowing that God has reservoirs of mercy meant to overcome our sin and heal our broken souls. The recognition of sin could be paralyzing, but it's not supposed to be, and God will not let us off the hook by claiming paralysis. Sin here is clearly a phenomenon of anthropology, a picture of the human; it is not a function of God's creative will. ■

Suggested Reading

Barth, *Karl Barth: Theologian of Freedom*, Green, ed.

Niebuhr, *The Children of Light and the Children of Darkness: A Vindication of Democracy and a Critique of Its Traditional Defense*.

Niebuhr, *The Nature and Destiny of Man*, vol. I, *Human Nature*.

Tillich, *Paul Tillich: Theologian of the Boundaries*, Taylor, ed.

Questions to Consider

1. What do you think are the most important similarities and differences among Tillich, Niebuhr, and Barth? What do they share that makes their accounts of evil similarly "Christian"? What important differences or disagreements exist among them?

2. Do you think Niebuhr is correct in claiming that sin is the only empirically verifiable doctrine? What role should experience play in judging our religious beliefs?

Post-WWII Roman Catholic Theology on Evil
Lecture 30

> **Sin would have to be terrifically bad and God would have to be immeasurably loving for God to come down to earth, undergo a human death on the cross, and descend into hell all in order to overcome humanity's estrangement from God. For von Balthasar, that, in fact, is what happened.**

In the 20th century, the Roman Catholic Church has made efforts to reach back into the tradition to uncover new resources to help people confront modern challenges. Evidence of these efforts is found in the theological reflections on hell by the Swiss theologian Hans Urs von Balthasar and in the mobilization of the category of "objectively evil acts" in papal teachings.

Von Balthasar was perhaps the most thoughtful and far-seeing Roman Catholic theologian of the 20th century. Most basically, he said that all Christians should pray that "all humans may be saved." According to von Balthasar, God clearly loves all humanity and wishes to save everyone from their own sin. Yet at the same time, God freely chooses to affirm human autonomy, especially the human's responsibility to accept salvation. Salvation encompasses the whole human, and thus, the whole human must participate in salvation. Those who do not make God's will for them their own will for themselves are destined to hell, defined as an utter separation from God.

Von Balthasar also said that we cannot know whether anyone—even Judas—has fully and finally rejected God. Because of this lack of knowledge on our part, we must acknowledge the real possibility of hell, especially for ourselves, but we are obligated by faith to hope that all may be saved. As evidence for this claim, von Balthasar points to two categories of scriptural passages in the New Testament that pertain to judgment and damnation. One of these speaks of individuals being condemned to eternal torment, and one expresses God's desire and ability to save all mankind. Our task is to acknowledge the tension between these two bodies of scriptural claims and hope, without presuming to know, that the claims that all can be saved theologically enframe the other claims about the potential for hell.

For von Balthasar, even sinners at the lowest depths of despair still find Christ with them and can walk out of hell with him, if only they will. The God who judges also accompanies the condemned to the seat of judgment and would stand in their stead to receive that judgment, again, if only the condemned will allow God to do so. It is a responsibility of everyone who properly thinks through the meaning of God's gift of salvation to humanity to understand that God's action is so powerful and so radical as to make salvation possible for every person. For von Balthasar, evil is an attempt to resist God's love, but we can hope that every being who is attempting to resist that love will one day give in, having realized that resistance is futile.

Killing even Hitler as a child to prevent the Holocaust and World War II would be evil because the actor would be taking the life of a small child.

In the 1990s, the language of intrinsic or objective evil began to appear in the discourse of the Catholic Church, particularly in the encyclicals of John Paul II. This pope was deeply concerned that the moral moorings of culture had been loosened in the late modern age, partially as a result of technology. Because humans can do so much more now than we used to be able to do, we increasingly bump up against the limits on what we ought to be able to do. John Paul saw the need to identify this temptation and resist it through the knowledge that certain things are intrinsically evil.

This language of objective moral evil focuses on the human capacity to engage in deliberate acts. In this understanding, acts are evil because of the circumstances surrounding them, because of the intention of the actor, or because an act is objectively evil. An act is objectively evil in one of two ways, the first of which is in its object, the most immediate result that the action seeks to achieve. Abortion is evil in the Catholic Church because the overt aim of the act is to end the life of a fetus. The second way in which an act can be intrinsically evil lies in the fact that its badness is wholly independent of the subjective attitude of the actor. Killing even Hitler as a child to prevent the Holocaust and World War II would be evil because the actor would be taking the life of a small child. In the language of the church, such an act "radically contradicts the good of the person made in God's image."

The language of an objectively evil act calls attention to increasingly powerful temptations in the modern world. Interestingly, this language has also moved from the realm of moral theology into that of social thought, that is, how the church speaks to society as a whole. Although it wasn't visible in much of the encyclical tradition before the 1980s, the language of intrinsic evil will likely be an important part of public discourse into the future. ■

Suggested Reading

Von Balthasar, *Dare We Hope That "All Men Be Saved"? with A Short Discourse on Hell*, Kipp and Krauth, trans.

Questions to Consider

1. Von Balthasar's emphasis on God's enduring love and the hope of salvation offers a compelling Christian response to the problem of evil. Yet as noted in the lecture, critics worry that von Balthasar risks downplaying evil's significance. Is von Balthasar's hope for universal salvation overly speculative and "other-worldly" or compelling and powerful?

2. Are some acts objectively evil—always wrong, no matter the circumstance or intention? Does the Roman Catholic concept of objectively evil acts help to clarify our moral judgment, or does it obscure the complexity of moral decision-making?

Post-WWII Jewish Thought on Evil
Lecture 31

The way we imagine the Shoah by and large today is that most people ... were killed in death camps and by industrial teams of the SS (the Nazi death guards). But this is, in fact, not true: Most of the victims—most of the Jews and other victims of the Shoah—were killed where they lived, almost at once by the German army when it came through.

At the end of the Second World War, the experience of the Shoah was one that most people simply could not process because they had no precedent for it. To think directly about the nature, meaning, and implications of this event has taken decades. In this lecture, we look at the work of four major Jewish thinkers on this issue: Richard Rubenstein, Arthur Cohen, Emil Fackenheim, and Emmanuel Levinas.

Richard Rubenstein is a living American philosopher and the author of the first book to explore the implications of the Shoah for Judaism from inside the Jewish faith (*After Auschwitz*). For traditional Rabbinic Judaism, Rubenstein argued, the Shoah must be understood either as a punishment or a complete mystery. He chooses the latter and claims that this mystery reveals the bankruptcy of some traditional Jewish understandings of God.

Rubenstein's argument is simple: to posit a just and omnipotent God who is in covenant with the people Israel and governing their fate and the fate of the world entails affirming that this God willed the murder of 12 million people. No one in his right mind would affirm that directly. Therefore, Rubenstein argues, the God of the traditional Jewish faith must be, effectively, dead. Furthermore, Rubenstein suggests that the Shoah reveals that the people Israel are not the chosen of God. Though Jewish rituals and practices have meaning and purpose, ultimately, the Shoah breaks apart any living relationship modern Jews could have with traditional Judaism. Jews should not, however, stop being Jews. Instead, they need to engage in a profound questioning of what God is doing now—if there is a God—and what the people Israel should do in the wake of Yahweh's demise. To reject the identity of the Jew is to continue the defeat that the Shoah represents of much of the people Israel.

One of the most interesting responses to Rubenstein was that of the American writer and philosopher Arthur Cohen. He saw the Nazi death camps as profane sites of anti-holiness, revealing a new kind of evil; this new evil is the *tremendum*, meaning both "the terror" and "the awesome." Cohen asserts that we must see the reality of the Shoah for what it represents, not simply treat it as continuous with other anti-Semitic pogroms. For Cohen, there is no "moral" to the story of the Shoah; it is an utter break with the past. He further believes that "God's silence is divine acquiescence in the work of murder and destruction." Because of this, Jews can break the bond with God; the *tremendum* has torn the covenant asunder. The God that the people Israel have worshiped is not the true Yahweh but an idol of their own fabrication.

Digital Stock.

For Cohen, the crucial thing to take from the Shoah is that we must see the reality of the camps for what they represent: a profound and profane series of sites of anti-holiness—a new kind of evil, the *tremendum*.

The God that Cohen wants the Jews to profess is more of a promise at present, not fully realized.

Emil Fackenheim, the third of our thinkers, experienced the Shoah firsthand. In his work *To Mend the World*, he asks what it means to be a Jew after the Holocaust. His answer is that the Jew is one who, without the historical accident of Hitler's losing the war, would be dead or would never have been born. In light of this new identity, Jews must undertake again the Jewish practice of *tikkun olam*, Hebrew words that mean "to mend the world." Among other things, the Jewish people must practice resistance to the aim of the Shoah, which was annihilation of the Jews. This annihilation would destroy the link between the God who will redeem the world through the Jewish people and a world that desperately needs redemption. To mend the world, Jews must recover the past of the Jewish tradition, recover from the trauma of the Shoah, and reconstitute their people. Fackenheim deems these obligations in the healing of the world the "614th commandment."

Emmanuel Levinas was another survivor of the Shoah and went on to become an incredible intellectual presence in the world. For Levinas, evil is suffering, and suffering is the transformation into passivity experienced by agents in the world through the actions of others. Evil affirms the presence of its victim no further than it needs the victim's existence in order to annihilate it. This kind of evil, Levinas thinks, is radically gratuitous, and the suffering it promotes is radically meaningless. Such suffering cannot be made useful for us. In fact, pain and suffering are, for Levinas, precisely the opposite of meaning; they are the annihilation of meaning. In the wake of Auschwitz, Levinas says that all people must care for one another. We must seek out those situations where people are being annihilated in this way and do what we can to stop it. It is only through that effort to stop suffering that any of our sufferings will ever have meaning. ∎

Suggested Reading

Morgan, ed., *A Holocaust Reader: Responses to the Nazi Extermination*.

Roth and Berenbaum, *Holocaust: Religious and Philosophical Implications*.

1. Arthur Cohen stressed that the Shoah was a new kind of horror and not merely another expression of anti-Semitism. Do you think the Shoah is a totally unique experience of evil? Should the Shoah change fundamentally the way we view the problem of evil?

2. Does the Jewish experience of the Shoah offer a unique perspective for viewing the nature of evil? And might the particularity of this experience offer Judaism a particularly privileged view of evil?

Arendt—The Banality of Evil
Lecture 32

The dark discovery of the 20th century is that humans are far more plastic than we heretofore imagined. People in a totalitarian state are turned into zombies, again, or robots that annihilate themselves and one another, all in the interest of the abstract totalitarian state.

Hannah Arendt, one of the most innovative thinkers of the 20th century, gave us two concepts that are important for thinking about evil in its political dimensions: totalitarianism and the banality of evil. For Arendt, the dangerous innovation of evil in the 20th century is the capacity of states to make people who would never normally be capable of cruelty to others become actors who play significant roles in vast schemes of human annihilation.

In her book *The Origins of Totalitarianism*, Arendt argued that modern totalitarian states, such as Nazi Germany, effectively embody a new kind of radical evil. Arendt believed that the totalitarian state is aptly named because it demands the totality of all that is within its boundaries—the products, culture, bodies, and souls of its citizens. It seeks to control education, technology, media, and industry in order to directly shape humans. Ultimately, Arendt thinks, this means that the totalitarian state is hostile to the idiosyncratic individuality of human beings and to human freedom. Such a regime's project inevitably entails the destruction of the human's capacity to be genuinely human.

About 10 years after the publication of *The Origins of Totalitarianism*, Arendt attended the trial of Adolf Eichmann in Jerusalem; from this experience, she compiled her most controversial book, *Eichmann in Jerusalem: A Report on the Banality of Evil*. Where earlier Arendt had described totalitarian evil as radical, in the character of Eichmann, she saw it as banal. As savagely efficient as Eichmann was, there was nothing demonic about him. Further, Arendt challenged the moral and legal concepts that organized the war crimes trials. To judge evil at the level of the Holocaust on the old moral concepts of individual responsibility, personal integrity, and individual intents is cowardly and dangerous, and it avoids the fundamental philosophical challenges the Holocaust presented. Arendt saw the need for us to rethink our understanding of how individual moral awareness can be warped by a society-wide moral change and to realize that warping is possible only because of a certain superficiality to most people's moral character.

In Arendt's view, Eichmann made the decision to continue shipping Jews to the death camps at the end of the war not because he was a demon, but because he believed himself to be doing his duty, which in his mind, went beyond mere obedience. In other words, Eichmann retained the language of morality even while horribly misdirecting its aims. Heinrich Himmler's 1943 speech to a group of SS leaders provides evidence for Arendt's view. Himmler assured his audience that despite what *they had gone through* in exterminating Jews, they had remained "decent" and had become "tough."

In other words, Eichmann retained the language of morality even while horribly misdirecting its aims.

Arendt's point is that a society can experience not just a moral collapse but a kind of moral inversion, in which the form of morality—the language of duty, honor, conscience, right and wrong—is retained even as the content—the actual meaning of those terms—is utterly inverted. In her summary of what happened to morality in the Third Reich, Arendt says, "Evil in the Third Reich had lost the quality by which most people recognize it—the quality of temptation." In fact, Arendt suggests, temptation flipped its place in our moral experience of the world. The law told us to kill, so we began to experience the desire not to kill as a temptation, and temptations—from a moral standpoint—should always be resisted.

To call those who carried out the Holocaust demons is wrong because it both offers them an odd sort of compliment and provides us with a subtle form of consolation. It compliments participants by according them qualities of demonic magnificence that their characters do not evidence. And it consoles us by giving us a framework to comprehend figures like Eichmann, when in fact, that framework is shattered by the reality of who such people really were. The Holocaust was not just an example of people gone villainous;

it was, instead, a society lapsing into an insane form of moral stupor—the banality of evil. For Arendt, the Holocaust wasn't a conspiracy of satanic supermen; it was an essentially bureaucratic phenomenon, and this was the problem that wasn't addressed in the trial of Eichmann.

To call the totalitarian evil of the Nazi regime "banal" doesn't make it trivial; it brings to our attention the challenge of a new kind of evil in a world filled with totalitarian states—the kind of ordinary evil that Eichmann represented. Since the trial of Eichmann, history has shown that the lessons of Arendt have yet to be learned. ■

Name to Know

Arendt, Hannah (1906–1975 C.E.). Born to a Jewish family in Königsberg, the birthplace of Immanuel Kant. She studied philosophy with Martin Heidegger, with whom she had an affair, and Karl Jaspers.

Suggested Reading

Arendt, *The Origins of Totalitarianism.*

Browning, *Ordinary Men: Reserve Police Battalion 101 and the Final Solution in Poland.*

Questions to Consider

1. Arendt worried about the modern state's "totalitarian" demands and understood the threat of totalitarianism as the most important threat to human life in the modern world. Does totalitarianism continue to exist as the preeminent danger in our world, or have other dangers supplanted this one as the most significant threat to human flourishing?

2. Arendt's insights concerning the "banality of evil" in many ways echo earlier concerns over the camouflaged character of evil, though Arendt reformulates this worry in a distinctively modern way. Is our age, more than others, prone to camouflaging or overlooking evil through bureaucracy, duty, or avoidance? Is evil today truly banal?

Life in Truth—20ᵗʰ-Century Poets on Evil
Lecture 33

> That phrase—"*Hier is kein warum*," "Here is no why"—captures a certain kind of dimension of the death camps in a way that, for [Primo] Levi and for those who survived them, is essential to their experience, if not—if we can use the word—meaning.

The master genre of literary thinking about evil in the century or so before World War II was the novel, but since that time, more potent explorations of evil have been found in memoirs, essays, and lyric poetry. But such genres as these face two fundamental problems that complicate their success: the aesthetic problem that it is somehow improper to write poetry or seek beauty in the wake of the events of World War II and the more generic challenge of representation. How can the truth be told about such events when the reality of them seems to dwarf the human capacity to represent and comprehend the magnitude of what happened?

Paul Celan was a survivor of the Shoah who discounted the idea that the act of writing poetry after Auschwitz seemed somehow barbaric. In fact, Celan wrote poetry *about* Auschwitz and in German. For him, the point of poetry is to get at the truth of things, and if the truth is evil and suffering, even if it's in the voice of those who caused the suffering, it must be spoken. Perhaps the most powerful poetic representation of the Shoah is Celan's "*Todesfuge*," or "Death Fugue." Recall that a fugue is a musical piece that repeats itself cyclically before coming together in a resolution at the end. Celan's fugue, however, breaks apart at the end. The final stanza is composed almost entirely of fragments of earlier lines of the poem but now ominously enjambed and unable to communicate any coherent message. The experience of the camp, Celan suggests, is beyond time and beyond logic.

Czeslaw Milosz was a member of the Polish resistance army during the war and the cultural attaché for the new communist Polish government afterward. He later defected, lived in the United States for a time, and won the Nobel Prize for literature. Milosz believed strongly in the power of language to call our attention to facts and truths that we would rather not recognize. In such works as "A Poem for the End of the World" or "A Poor Christian Looks at the Ghetto," Milosz speaks with a profound directness about events taking place in front of his eyes.

In "A Poem for the End of the Century," Milosz seems to be troubled by the naivety of the postwar idea that evil has been vanquished. He suggests that his opinion is "a bit shameful," but he's compelled to think such thoughts and speak them by his own memories of suffering and death—both the suffering and death that he personally experienced and the suffering and death of Jesus. For Milosz, Jesus was both temporal and eternal, suggesting that the events of the 20th century spoke to something more perennial than just that time. Milosz says that at the heart of everything, perhaps, is a reality "of pain and also guilt / in the structure of the world." Given that, can we really believe that evil has been forever overcome? He ends the poem by saying that his concerns are "not for people" and that the postwar world is genuinely "blessed." The point seems to be that goodness is good in itself, even if not everyone can share in it.

> **[Zbigniew Herbert's] poems read like telegrams sent from some desperate city, fighting off an almost insuperable army.**

In his poetry, Zbigniew Herbert is far more ironic, epigrammatic, and terse than his countryman Milosz. His poems read like telegrams sent from some desperate city, fighting off an almost insuperable army. Like Milosz, Herbert was a veteran of the Polish resistance army, and his poetry later became one of the inspirations for the Solidarity movement. Each word in Herbert's poems carries immense weight, but each also stands stripped of some essential ease about its meaning, lending his poems a sense of urgency. As he says in "The Envoy of Mr. Cogito," "you have little time you must give testimony." The overall impression of Herbert's poetry is one of ironic truth-telling against tremendous odds, offering us a powerful rhetoric by which to resist the attempt of the totalitarian state to lie to us constantly.

Probably Herbert's most directly relevant poem for us is one entitled "The Power of Taste." In it, he says that resisting totalitarian regimes "didn't require great character at all"; it required only taste. The ugliness of totalitarianism—"a home-brewed Mephisto in a Lenin jacket," "boys with potato faces"—could be resisted by someone with a proper sense of beauty. The ability to recognize beauty is a structure of the conscience that helps us sustain our moral stance in the world and, in the end, is the consummate way to resist evil. For Herbert, not to write poetry after Auschwitz would be to refuse to try to recover something of civilization and humanity in the wake of that horror. ∎

Suggested Reading

Milosz, *The Captive Mind*, Zielonko, trans.

Weissbort, ed., *The Poetry of Survival: Post-War Poets of Central and Eastern Europe.*

Questions to Consider

1. In their own distinct ways, each of the authors in this lecture attempts to describe something of the nature of evil, yet each also suggests to us that the medium of poetry can help to illumine in ways that other kinds of words cannot. Does the medium matter when discussing the nature of evil? Are certain kinds of language (poetry or literature, for example) capable of revealing things that other mediums do not?

2. In what ways does the problem of evil reveal the limits of language? Can evil ever be adequately described or understood in human words?

Science and the Empirical Study of Evil
Lecture 34

> The [Good Samaritan] study uses the biblical story perhaps most profoundly anathema to its findings as a core component of its experiment—it's almost as if these psychologists were guided by Satan or something. It's just such a perfect example of why exactly the Good Samaritan story needs to be still listened to by many Christians.

Since World War II, social scientists have developed various experiments to attempt to measure the human's tendencies toward blind obedience or willful engagement in inflicting cruelty on others. In this lecture, we'll look at three such experiments: the famous Milgram experiments on obedience to authority, Philip Zimbardo's notorious Stanford prison experiment, and the disturbing series of Good Samaritan studies run at Princeton Theological Seminary.

In 1961, Stanley Milgram, a psychologist at Yale University, conducted a series of experiments designed to highlight the power of authority. Subjects were recruited to administer a series of electric shocks of escalating voltage to victims strapped to a chair in another room, out of sight but not out of hearing. As the subjects thought they were giving the victims increasingly powerful shocks, a tape recorder in the other room played a series of desperate cries while an actor banged on a wall, then fell ominously silent as the shocks rose above a certain level. Ultimately, the subjects were directed to give three 450-volt shocks in succession to the now-silent victim.

In Milgram's first set of experiments, 65 percent of participants delivered the final series of shocks, though many were very uncomfortable doing so. At some point, every participant paused and questioned the experiment. Only 1 participant out of 40 steadfastly refused to administer shocks above the 300-volt level. Later studies showed that roughly two-thirds of all participants inflicted what they thought to be fatal voltages under orders from the experimenter. Although Milgram's experiment is contested, it points to a disquieting aspect of the behavior of ordinary people in modern industrial society.

Another psychology professor, Philip Zimbardo of Stanford, explored humans' tendencies toward brutality in the Stanford prison experiment. Here, 21 undergraduates deemed psychologically stable were chosen to act as guards and prisoners in a mock prison. The guards were given uniforms, mirrored sunglasses, and wooden batons, meant to be worn only to signify that they were guards. The prisoners were given ill-fitting smocks and stocking caps, were called by assigned numbers, and wore chains around their ankles. All participants understood that they were taking part in an experiment.

The prisoners were "arrested" at their homes, then brought to the mock prison, where the guards quickly lived into their roles to a much greater degree than was anticipated. From the first day, they enjoyed demonstrating their status to the prisoners and, by the end of the experiment, roughly one-third of them showed clear sadistic tendencies; that is, they clearly enjoyed inflicting pain and got pleasure from the infliction of pain itself, no matter that it led to other benefits for them.

Dover Pictorial Archive Series.

Studies, including those based on the Good Samaritan parable, have drawn some scientists to the situational attribution theory, which says people are much more determined by their surrounding context than their innate character.

Zimbardo and others have argued that the experiment suggests not a "lord of the flies" mentality among humans but the malleability of the human personality, that is, how readily we inhabit a role when we are provided with a rationale for it and a suitable set of surrounding social structures. Zimbardo and his team believed the experiment revealed that people are inherently creatures of context, even if that context is temporary and, perhaps, implausible.

Zimbardo's experiment showed how easy it is for humans to slip into the grip of sadism; equally troubling, the Good Samaritan studies, conducted by John Darley and Daniel Batson at Princeton University, showed how easy it is for people to be lured away from goodness by even trivial circumstances. These studies involved groups of seminary students asked to give a talk either about the parable of the Good Samaritan or about job opportunities in a seminary. Some were told that they had to hurry across campus to give the talk, while others were not told to hurry. On the way to the lecture site, all the students passed by a person slumped in an alleyway, obviously in need of help. As you might guess, the depressing conclusion was that the students who had been studying the Good Samaritan story did not stop any more often than the ones preparing for a speech on job opportunities. If they were in a hurry, only about 10 percent would stop to give aid, even when they were on their way to deliver a sermon about the Good Samaritan.

All these studies point to the conclusions of situational attribution theory, according to which people's behavior is more determined by their surrounding context than their innate character. Character, as an innate moral quality we possess, is not so important as we might think; perhaps it's not even real. However, it's also true that in the right context, people can be better than we anticipate; they can possibly find the resources within themselves to be moral. Perhaps in coming decades, psychologists will find ways to explore how people can learn to help one another and to resist evil. ■

Suggested Reading

Milgram, *Obedience to Authority*.

1. Modern experimentation has suggested that context is key in guiding human behavior, toward both good and evil acts. How might this suggestion change our conception of the relation between evil and human character? Is context the key to improving an evil character or corrupting a good one?

2. What is the usefulness of science in understanding evil? Can science play a role in helping us to combat or control evil, or is evil something that lies somehow beyond the realm of science?

The "Unnaming" of Evil
Lecture 35

After 9/11, ... we seemed forced to choose between either a language of evil that provides a kind of inadvertent metaphysical compliment to bad people by calling them "evil" (in a way that makes Osama bin Laden sound like Darth Vader) or a language of intelligible or at least explainable motivations that forbids [us] from talking about bad people as bad, ... but just misunderstood.

A general theme for these lectures, especially the ones covering the 20th century, has been a deepening sense of the disparity between our thinking about evil, historically and today, and the realities that that thinking is meant to represent and help us respond to. From Joseph Conrad to Freud to Hannah Arendt, we've seen a growing unease in these lectures about our capacity to grasp and communicate the reality of evil. It's also true that this is, in some ways, an old theme, stretching back to the *Epic of Gilgamesh* and Genesis. Nonetheless, contemporary thinkers seem to be explicitly concerned with whether or not our power has outstripped our wisdom.

The philosopher Michel Foucault said, "For centuries, humanity had been what Aristotle had said we were: a natural animal with a political situation that it had to work out. But now we are an animal whose politics put our very natural survival into question." That fact is new in the past century or so and gives rise to a cluster of anxieties: about genocide, scientific and technological developments, and the changing nature of culture and society in general. The question we face today is whether our new situation is really amenable to treatment and understanding by the traditional resources we use to understand and respond to evil.

One dimension of this question is seen in the concerns of scientists, from those associated with the Manhattan Project forward. J. Robert Oppenheimer, technical director of the Manhattan Project, made an exemplary statement about science struggling with its moral implications in the wake of World War II: "In some sort of crude sense, which no vulgarity, no humor, no overstatement can quite extinguish, the physicists have known sin; and this is a knowledge which they cannot lose." The knowledge these scientists used had been meant for healing and improvement of life, but it had now been turned to purposes of annihilation. In the past 50 years or so, with germlines, DNA modifications, and other "advancements," the potential exists for science to be even more destructive than it was with the development of nuclear weapons.

We are a nation that seems serially to obliterate the dark lessons of the past, and this does not seem to be our problem alone.

Another body of thinkers and writers, especially journalists, who wonder whether we have learned anything about evil since World War II is those who have dealt with the history of genocide. Arendt had warned that the techniques of terror pioneered by the Nazis would be taken up and improved by others, and she has been proved right in such places as Cambodia, the former Yugoslavia, Rwanda, and the Sudan. Such genocidal events seem to explode into our consciousness as if they had come out of nowhere, but in retrospect, we discover similar patterns. Why is it so hard for us to name these realities and figure out how to stop them?

Over the past 20 years or so, a number of journalists have thought about this question and tried to come up with a template for identifying and resisting events of mass genocide. First, we must understand the reality of the situation as clearly as possible and resist the temptation to immediately fit it into received moral patterns. Then, we must communicate the facts we have discerned in a vivid and powerful way, although it may be difficult to convince others of the reality we have witnessed.

These two areas of concern—those about science and those about uncovering the realities of evil—reemerged after the events of September 11, 2001. In the aftermath of 9/11, many spoke of the loss of innocence for the United States, the loss of a naïve belief that the world was good. In thinking back over our history, however—the Civil War, the genocide against Native Americans, two world wars, Vietnam—one wonders how many times the United States can lose its innocence. We are a nation that seems serially to obliterate the dark lessons of the past, and this does not seem to be our problem alone. The crux of the problem in modern cultures seems to be that we lack both the language and the imagination to respond usefully to the challenge evil presents to our moral self-understanding.

Today, we imagine the world and people as basically ordered. This means that we imagine evil as the sudden and inexplicable eruption of malice and madness in an otherwise harmonious world. But genocide and other events of mass evil will always surprise us as long as we think that humans cannot be bad. This is not so much an understanding of evil as a failure to understand it. One solution to this failing is to explore humanity's thinking about evil in the past and to look for echoes that can be useful to our thinking in the modern world. ■

Suggested Reading

Mills and Brunner, eds., *The New Killing Fields: Massacre and the Politics of Invention.*

VanDeMark, Brian. *Pandora's Keepers: Nine Men and the Atomic Bomb.*

Questions to Consider

1. Oppenheimer noted that physicists had "known sin" in the creation of the atomic bomb. Have our other current technologies known sin in the same way? How has our growing knowledge and technical sophistication been complicit in evil, and how important is this complicity?

2. What conclusions ought we to draw from the persistence of genocide throughout the 20th century? Is genocide a particularly modern expression of evil? How should we situate these crimes in relation to others throughout history?

3. Do we have the resources to understand and respond to evil in the modern world? If so, what are these resources and how ought we to use them? If not, why not?

Where Can Hope Be Found?
Lecture 36

> One of the things that [entertainment] is most interested in is
> criminality, evil, malice, these sorts of things. The reason why? Because
> for us especially as moderns, as people here in the 21st century, it's hard
> for us to imagine a world where evil of our sort exists; we don't know
> what to do.

As we've seen throughout these lectures, evil is truly what Zbigniew
Herbert called the "dense and dark material" of history, and to shed
light on it requires many consciousnesses. But the fact that evil is a
difficult problem doesn't mean that we can't wrestle some comprehension
out of its mystery. The approaches we have explored to thinking about evil
offer us a good place to begin.

Over the course of these lectures, we've seen the manifold attempts by
thinkers and writers of diverse beliefs to represent and anatomize evil,
diagnose its challenges, and formulate responses, and certain themes appear
in this thinking repeatedly. Such thinkers as Plato, Augustine, and Pascal
believed that evil suggests a kind of nihilism—nothingness—in the world,
while Aristotle, Nietzsche, and Freud viewed evil as a natural component
of the world. Irenaeus, Hegel, and many contemporary thinkers imagine
evil as an inevitable step in the process of maturation for human beings
and, perhaps, the cosmos as a whole. We've also seen a longstanding debate
between thinkers about evil: Again, such thinkers as Plato, Augustine, and
Pascal see evil as the refusal to be properly extreme in the pursuit of virtue,
while others, such as Aristotle, Montaigne, and Hume, see a danger in the
expression of extremity.

The debates we've seen related to theodicy raised questions about the
implications of our understanding of evil for our understanding of the
universe and the reverse, that is, the implications of our understanding of the
universe for our understanding of evil. Another issue we've explored is the
relationship between civilization and barbarism. In the 20th century, Arendt
and others have argued that modernity itself is complicit in creating new

kinds of evil. The literature we've read—the work of Dante, Milton, Camus, and others—vividly captures the question that perhaps lies at the heart of thinking about evil: What is its fundamental character? Is it banal, empty, demonic? Is it unnatural to our cosmos or part of the world's essence?

The extent of malice in the 20th and 21st centuries has been truly remarkable, yet we generally think of ourselves as somehow in a better moral situation than people in previous centuries. Something like the Holocaust, for example, would have been unimaginable in the 18th century. The problem seems to be, as Andrew Delbanco said, that "a gap has opened up between our awareness of evil and the intellectual resources we have for handling it." Because we don't understand evil, we don't know how to resist it. Evil bewilders us, and our typical response to it is often a theatricalization that masks our incomprehension.

A more poignant, ironic joke on the part of whatever God may be is hard to imagine: that Western civilization has returned to fight in its birthplace.

It's stunning to think that American troops are now fighting in places that the Greeks and Romans fought 2,500 years ago. For some time in the last decade, the ruins of the ancient city of Babylon were within the perimeter of an American military base. A more poignant, ironic joke on the part of whatever God may be is hard to imagine: that Western civilization has returned to fight in its birthplace. It may be that the challenge of evil is just too hard for us, but we can't stop asking the questions. We know that evil isn't likely to go away, and even if we try to avoid it, it will loom on the edge of our consciousness and eventually intrude into our lives again.

We need a way of thinking about evil that will avoid two significant pitfalls: the attempt to demonize people who are unlike us and the temptation to internalize evil and paralyze us with guilt. These lectures have suggested several routes to a workable language of evil. Still, there is a latent time bomb here: Does the knowledge or insight we might gain about the problem produce anything like hope? Any answer to the problem of evil must recognize the thought that we may not be able, finally, to gain any useful insights about it.

It seems that all the evidence of evil, suffering, and cruelty in the world would not provoke us unless we felt that they were, in some fundamental way, wrong. The fact that evil is so puzzling and the fact that humans have persisted in our questioning of it seem themselves signs of hope. But we should not be self-congratulatory about our stubbornness in this arena. It's not a form of moral courage but a form of what we might call moral acknowledgment, of giving witness to what we see. Our reflection on evil doesn't begin from theoretical presuppositions or armchair philosophizing but by attending to our "pre-theoretical" responses to evil. We naturally resist evil—intellectually and practically—and in that resistance, we manifest some sense of goodness and justice. Perhaps a truly useful response to evil can be found in this practical resistance. ∎

Questions to Consider

1. Can you identify one aspect of the course or one insight into the nature of evil that you found especially compelling? What about this insight is significant for you and why?

2. What do you think Leonard Wolf was trying to say when he observed, "I'm planting iris and they will be flowering long after [Hitler] is dead"? What hopes are capable of sustaining us against evil, and how can we cultivate these?

Timeline

c. 2150–2000 B.C.E. .... Ancient Near Eastern
writings begin to appear.

c. 587–538.................................... Ancient Israelites exiled to
Mesopotamia in the Babylonian
Captivity; probable era in which the
book of Genesis was composed.

c. 538... Persians take control of the
Mediterranean world.

431–404 .... Peloponnesian War.

c. 428–347.................................... Plato lives and teaches in Athens.

c. 384–322.................................... Aristotle.

333... Alexander the Great defeats Darius III.

27... Octavian names himself Caesar
Augustus; Rome assumes control
of the Mediterranean world.

33 C.E. .... Jesus crucified outside
Jerusalem by the Romans.

c. 40–100....................................... New Testament composed.

70... Destruction of the Jerusalem
Temple by the Romans.

c. 177... Irenaeus becomes bishop of Lyon.

c. 200–500............................... Formation of the Talmud.

324... Constantine Christianizes
the Roman Empire.

354–430 .... Augustine of Hippo.

410... Rome sacked by Visigoths.

c. 570–632................................ Muhammad.

c. 644–652................................ Uthman, the third caliph,
canonizes the written Qu'ran.

1033–1109 .... Anselm of Canterbury.

1224–1275 .... St. Thomas Aquinas.

1265... Aquinas begins writing the
Summa Theologiae.

1265–1321 .... Dante Alighieri.

1308–1321 .... Dante writes his *Commedia*
(the "Divine Comedy").

1348... Black Death ravages Europe.

1453... Constantinople falls to the Ottomans.

1517... Martin Luther publishes his 95 theses;
Protestant Reformation begins.

1532... Machiavelli's *The Prince* is
published posthumously.

1588–1679 .... Thomas Hobbes.

1608–1674 .... John Milton.

1623–1662 .... Blaise Pascal.

1642–1651 .... English Civil War.

1651.. Hobbes publishes *Leviathan*.

1667.. Milton publishes *Paradise Lost*.

1670.. Pascal's *Pensées* published.

1710.. Gottfried Wilhelm Leibniz
publishes *Theodicy*.

1724–1804 .... Immanuel Kant.

1755.. Earthquake devastates Lisbon.

1770–1831 .... G. W. F. Hegel.

1775–1783 .... American Revolutionary War.

1793.. Kant writes *Religion within the
Boundaries of Mere Reason*.

1815.. Napoleon defeated at the
Battle of Waterloo.

1835–1910 .... Mark Twain (Samuel Clemens).

1844–1900 .... Friedrich Nietzsche.

1848.. Karl Marx publishes the
Communist Manifesto.

1856–1939 .... Sigmund Freud.

1861–1865 .... American Civil War.

1865 .... Lincoln's Second Inaugural Address.

1884 .... Mark Twain publishes *The Adventures of Huckleberry Finn*.

1886 .... Nietzsche's *Beyond Good and Evil* appears.

1906–1975 .... Hannah Arendt.

1913–1960 .... Albert Camus.

1914–1918 .... First World War.

1917 .... Bolshevik Revolution establishes communism in Russia.

1929 .... Freud writes *Civilization and Its Discontents*.

1939–1945 .... Nazis invade Poland, World War II.

1943 .... Heinrich Himmler delivers speech to his soldiers in Pozan.

1945 .... Auschwitz liberated by Soviet troops.

1945 .... The United States drops the first atomic bomb on Hiroshima.

1948 .... Albert Camus' *The Plague* appears.

1961 .... Trial of Adolph Eichmann in Jerusalem.

2001 .... Terrorists attack the World Trade Center.

Glossary

Abraham: Early patriarch of Israel whose story is recounted in Genesis. He makes a covenant with God and obediently follows God's command to sacrifice his son, Isaac, though God intervenes at the final moment.

akedah: Hebrew word meaning "binding," associated with the story of Abraham's obedient willingness to sacrifice Isaac and God's deliverance.

akrasia: An ancient Greek term that Aristotle uses for "weakness of will." Suggests an explanation for evil as a pathology of moral motivation, a divided, incoherent, or "weak" will.

Babel: In the book of Genesis, the site where humanity attempts to construct a tower to heaven; often associated with Mesopotamian Babylon. The story describes evil as overt rebellion against God and suggests a link between evil and "empire" that carries over into the Christian New Testament.

Cain and Abel: Sons of Adam and Eve in Genesis. The story recounts the murder of Abel by his brother, Cain, after God shows favor to Abel. Suggests that evil is now a permanent feature of human life that must be struggled against.

contrapasso: Theme in Dante's *Inferno* that emphasizes the continuity between sin and punishment in hell. Suggests a notion of hell as intrinsic punishment, in which punishment is a constitutive part of the nature of evil.

das Nichtige: Karl Barth's term to describe "the nothing," a force in excess of human wrongdoing that threatens everything that exists and undergirds sin. Barth uses the term to stress evil's unreality but also its profundity and depth.

death drive: Term used by Sigmund Freud to describe the instinct opposite to Eros in the human psyche that seeks to dissolve the world back into a primeval, inorganic state. The concept denies that evil can be explained rationally and introduces guilt into the human psyche.

divertissements: Term meaning "diversions" used by Blaise Pascal to describe a way of being in the world aimed at avoiding the facts of one's existence, especially the fact of death.

Enuma Elish: Babylonian creation myth, in which the god Marduk establishes himself as king over the gods by defeating Tiamat, the chaos monster.

Genesis: First book of the Jewish and Christian Scriptures, which tells the story of God's creation of the world, the origin of evil, and the development of the people Israel. Includes the stories of Adam and Eve, Cain and Abel, and Abraham and Isaac.

Gilgamesh: Important surviving work from Mesopotamia in the 3rd millennium B.C.E., in which the hero, Gilgamesh, suffers as he searches for immortality and founds a city. An important early text to understand a world where suffering occurs.

Hinneni: Hebrew word often translated "Here I am." Appears throughout the Hebrew Bible and Old Testament to denote a posture of attentiveness and obedience. Used by both Abraham and Samuel when each receives a call from God.

Iblis: Rebellious angel in the Qur'an, later associated with Satan. Refuses to obey God's command to "bow down" before Adam, and from this refusal, all evil proceeds. His story displays a connection between evil and moral rectitude; in the Sufi tradition, evil grows out of Iblis's scrupulous monotheism. Later characterizations of Iblis stress both evil's personal and impersonal character.

Job: Book of the Hebrew Bible and Old Testament that recounts the story of Job, a righteous man who is tested by God. The text is famous for its focus on the non-explicability of evil and suffering.

Oedipus Rex: Greek tragedy written by Sophocles, an Athenian tragedian. The drama tells the story of Oedipus, the king of Thebes, who unknowingly murders his father, Laius, and sleeps with his mother, Jocasta. Highlights the relationship between evil and tragedy in Greek thought.

original sin: Christian doctrine that stresses evil as dramatic, powerful, and endemic to the human condition. Presented in limited form in the New Testament and later developed by such Christian theologians as Augustine of Hippo.

Paradise Lost: Epic poem composed by John Milton, an English poet in the 17th century. The poem tells the story of the Fall of Adam and Eve; it is especially famous for its compelling treatment of Satan.

The Peloponnesian War: A historical work written by Thucydides, recounting the war between the Greek city-state of Athens and its rival, Sparta. Includes the story of Athens' turn of fortunes following its cruelty to the Melians and suggests the lack of straightforward moral order in the world.

pleasure principle: Term coined by Sigmund Freud to describe our desire to be happy and feel pleasure, while acknowledging that happiness is not a normal state of human life. The pleasure principle leads to the sublimation of our desires in order to achieve relative happiness.

Qur'an: Sacred text of Islam, literally meaning the "recitation." Contains the revelation according to Muhammad, transmitted to him by Gabriel.

Rabbinic Judaism: Form of Jewish faith and practice that flourished from the 3rd century C.E., the era of the composition of the Talmud, to the present. It takes Talmud to be an authority in interpretation of the Torah. This tradition offers a picture of evil in mundane terms.

radical evil: The term used by Immanuel Kant to describe the fundamental disposition of the will to privilege itself over the general good. The term stresses the idea that evil's resolution must go beyond cognition to a transformation of character itself.

Revelation: Apocalyptic text contained in the New Testament that describes the final cosmic battle between God and the forces of evil. Stresses the conception of evil as a cosmic struggle that must be patiently endured until conquered by God.

Shoah: Hebrew word meaning "catastrophe," now often used to describe the Holocaust.

yetzer ha ra: Hebrew term meaning "evil impulse." Key term in discussions of evil by Rabbinic Judaism; stresses evil as a part of humanity's created nature and rooted in self-interest. Leads to a vision of evil as less a cosmic struggle than a practical challenge.

Biographical Notes

Alighieri, Dante (c. 1265–1321 C.E.). Born in Florence, Italy, to a prominent family. Like many of his contemporaries, Dante was thoroughly involved in the controversy between the Guelphs and the Ghibellines, two factions associated with the papacy and the Holy Roman Empire in a struggle for political prominence. Dante was a moderate member of the Guelph party; after the triumph of his political enemies among the more extreme Guelphs, Dante was exiled from Florence for life while he was in Rome on an embassy. He never saw Florence again. Afterward, he began to write the *Commedia*, a poem that recounts Dante's journey through heaven, hell, and purgatory. *The Inferno*, one section of the *Commedia*, became one of the most important depictions of hell in the Western imagination. Dante's body still rests in Ravenna, in exile from the Florence that he loved; the sentence of death the Florence City Council had laid down upon him during his life was at last revoked by that Council, by a vote of 19 to 5, in 2008.

Aquinas, Thomas (1225–1274 C.E.). Born to a prominent family in Aquino in southern Italy. At the age of 19, Aquinas expressed a desire to join the monastic order of the Dominicans, but his family opposed this decision and locked him in a castle for two years. During this time, his family made every attempt to dissuade him from his decision, at one point even hiring a prostitute to convince Aquinas to renounce his celibacy. Eventually, however, his family relented and Aquinas joined the Dominican order. He moved to Paris, where he became a professor of theology. He eventually moved to Rome, where he began work on his *Summa Theologiae*, arguably the most important work in medieval theology and one of the most important in the history of Western Christianity. Near the end of his life, Aquinas had a series of experiences that made him stop writing; when asked why he had stopped, he replied that, compared to what he had now experienced, "all I have written is straw." Having written more than 10,000 pages, he died when he was not yet 50.

Arendt, Hannah (1906–1975 C.E.). Born to a Jewish family in Königsberg, the birthplace of Immanuel Kant. She studied philosophy with Martin Heidegger, with whom she had an affair, and Karl Jaspers. Arendt completed a dissertation on Augustine but was prevented from continuing in academia because she was Jewish. To escape Nazi persecution, in 1933, Arendt fled to France, then in 1940, to America, where she became a prominent intellectual in New York City. She published *On the Origins of Totalitarianism*, a famous work analyzing the nature of totalitarian regimes. She also reported on the trial of Adolf Eichmann for the *New Yorker*, later transforming her work into *Eichmann in Jerusalem: A Study on the Banality of Evil*. Arendt had a distinguished academic career and taught at numerous institutions before becoming the first female professor to teach at Princeton University. She is now recognized as one of the most important philosophers of the 20th century.

Aristotle (384–322 B.C.E.). Born in Stageira as a member of the aristocracy. Eventually, Aristotle made his way to Athens, became a disciple of Plato, and studied at Plato's Academy for almost 20 years. Following his departure from the Academy, he was invited by Philip II of Macedon to become the tutor of Philip's son, Alexander the Great. Aristotle later returned to Athens to found his own school, the Lyceum. Like Plato, Aristotle wrote dialogues, but none has survived. Many of Aristotle's most important works are thought to be lecture notes taken by his students.

Augustine of Hippo (354–430 C.E.). Sometimes called the "second founder of the faith," Augustine is commonly recognized as one of the most important figures in Western Christianity. He was born in Thagasate, a Roman city in North Africa. He studied rhetoric and eventually moved to Carthage. There, he began to live an increasingly hedonistic lifestyle and became involved with the Manicheans, a religious sect that divided the world dualistically into good and evil. At the age of 30, Augustine moved to Milan to occupy a prestigious chair in rhetoric. During this period, he moved away from Manicheanism and eventually converted to Christianity. With his conversion, Augustine gave up his career in rhetoric and later returned to Africa, where he founded a semi-formal monastery with friends. On a visit to Hippo, he was forced to become a priest and bishop-in-waiting of the town. He wrote a large number of highly influential works, including *Confessions* and *The City of God.*

Calvin, Jean (1509–1564 C.E.). Calvin was born in France and studied philosophy and law. He was strongly influenced by French humanism and was eventually forced to flee France because of his call for Catholic reforms. In 1536, Calvin published the first edition of *Institutes of the Christian Religion*, a key text of the Protestant Reformation, and eventually made Geneva a center of the movement. Historically, Calvin's reforms and the community in Geneva are the origin of the Presbyterian Church. Calvin outlived his wife and all his children, and—to protect against people seeking relics—he was buried in an unmarked grave in the Geneva cemetery.

Conrad, Joseph (1857–1924 C.E.). Born to a noble Polish family under the name of Józef Teodor Konrad Korzeniowsk. Conrad was orphaned at the age of 11, after his mother and father died of sickness. He became a seaman at the age of 16 and spent several years sailing around the world on both legal and illegal ventures. He eventually assumed the position of captain aboard a steamship in the Congo, and this experience became the basis of *Heart of Darkness.* Owing to failing health and the desire to write, Conrad settled in Essex, England, where he became one of the great modern novelists and a narrator of stories hard to tell over high tea.

Dostoevsky, Fyodor (1821–1881 C.E.). The son of a violent alcoholic, a former military surgeon who practiced at a hospital for the poor in Moscow. His mother died when he was 16, and his father died two years later, possibly murdered by his serfs. Dostoevsky was subject to epilepsy fits from the age of 9, but he attended military school despite his ailments. He soon began to write but was imprisoned and sentenced to death for his involvement with Petrashevsky Circle, a radical literary group. He endured a mock execution before a firing squad and was sent to a prison camp in Siberia. Following his release, Dostoevsky was forced to serve several years in a Siberian military regiment. He wrote prolifically for the remainder of his life, and his works are commonly recognized as masterpieces of Russian and world literature.

Freud, Sigmund (1856–1939 C.E.). Born in Píbor, a village in the Austro-Hungarian Empire, to poor Jewish parents, who sacrificed to provide their son with an excellent education. The family eventually moved to Vienna, where Freud studied and, later, joined the medical faculty at the University of Vienna. He began to experiment with hypnosis but soon abandoned this method in favor of discussions meant to unlock the unconscious. Freud began to publish his ideas in the 1900s and soon developed a following in psychological circles. His fame continued to spread through and after the First World War. In 1932, he received the prestigious Goethe prize for his contributions to German culture, but in 1933, the Nazis took control of Germany and designated Freud's books to be banned and burned. Freud and his family went into hiding and eventually escaped to England; four of Freud's sisters, however, died in concentration camps. He himself died in September of 1939, worried that, in the struggle through world history of the titans—the death drive and the love drive—the death drive had finally won.

Hegel, G. W. F. (1770–1831 C.E.). Born in Stuttgart, Germany. When he was 13, his mother died of fever, which Hegel and his father both caught and barely survived. After completing his early education, Hegel enrolled at the seminary in Tübingen, where he became friends with Friedrich Schelling, later a well-known philosopher. Hegel worked as a private tutor before becoming a professor at the university in Jena, where he witnessed Napoleon Bonaparte, after a battle, cantering through the streets on horseback. Eventually, Hegel became widely recognized for his work *The Phenomenology of Spirit* and was appointed to the prestigious chair in philosophy at the University of Berlin. Hegel is best known as a key figure in German idealism, a movement that stressed the importance of ideas and the mind as driving forces in history. Hegel's philosophy is also known as one of the most important reactions to Immanuel Kant and was highly influential on Karl Marx.

Hobbes, Thomas (1588–1679 C.E.). Born in Wiltshire, England—supposedly when his mother heard news of the first sighting of the Spanish Armada—and educated at Oxford. He began his academic career by translating Thucydides's *The Peloponnesian War*, the first translation of that work ever attempted in English. During the English Civil War, Hobbes moved to France and composed *Leviathan*, a political treatise that argued for the legitimacy of governments on the basis of social contract and the supremacy of sovereign authority.

Irenaeus of Lyon (c. 150–c. 202 C.E.). Irenaeus was probably born in Smyrna and raised by Christian parents. During the persecution of Christians by Marcus Aurelius, Irenaeus was imprisoned for his faith, and he eventually became the second bishop of Lyon. During his tenure as a bishop, Irenaeus composed "Against Heresies," a famous Christian apologetic work against Gnosticism. He was also the first church father to attest to the validity of the four Gospels that later became part of the New Testament.

Kant, Immanuel (1724–1804 C.E.). Born in Königsberg, Prussia, where he lived all his life. A student at the University of Königsberg, Kant made several important contributions to astronomy in his early career before turning increasingly to philosophy. In 1781, after almost a decade of silence since becoming a professor at the university, Kant published the *Critique of Pure Reason*, a work widely regarded as one of the most important in the history of philosophy. He went on, over the next 20 years, to revolutionize philosophy in many ways. Kant is most famous for arguing that causality, time, and space are not the products of empirical observation; rather, he said, they are structures built into the nature of reason itself. Likewise, Kant's moral philosophy, especially his *Groundwork for the Metaphysics of Morals*, has been highly influential in Western thought. Kant died in Königsberg, having never traveled more than 100 miles from that city.

Luther, Martin (1483–1546 C.E.). Born in Eisleben, Germany, a city that was then part of the Holy Roman Empire. Luther briefly studied law but became a monk in the Augustinian order after making a vow during a lightning storm. Eventually, Luther began to teach theology at the University of Wittenberg, where he famously published his 95 Theses protesting the church's sale of indulgences in 1517. His dispute with Pope Leo X resulted in Luther's excommunication and the beginning of the Protestant Reformation. Theologically, Luther's most important claim was his emphasis on justification by faith—the insistence that human beings are saved by God on the basis of grace alone, apart from any righteous works.

Machiavelli, Niccolo (1469–1527 C.E.). Born in Florence, Italy, where he received a classical education and training in service to the Florentine state. Machiavelli became Second Chancellor of the Republic of Florence, in charge of managing foreign affairs and the militia. With the triumph of his political enemies, he was tortured and exiled from Florence. He was the author of *The Prince*, a political treatise for rulers that argued that moral perfection cannot govern the world, especially in politics. Machiavelli is considered by many to be the first political "realist."

Marx, Karl (1818–1883 C.E.). Born and educated in Trier, Germany. He enrolled at the University of Bonn but later transferred to the University of Berlin. There, Marx encountered the Young Hegelians, a group of thinkers who advocated for radical political proposals in conversation with Hegelian philosophy. Marx was influenced by this movement, though he also began to develop his own account of "dialectical materialism." He soon traveled to Paris, where he met his lifelong friend, Friedrich Engels. Eventually, Marx and Engels published *The Communist Manifesto*, a radical political tract that attacked capitalism and characterized history as the development of class struggle. Following its publication, Marx moved to London, where he remained until his death, struggling with ill health and in conditions of near poverty for himself and his family. He never stopped predicting the eventual communist revolution, which he was convinced would begin in either England or Germany.

Milton, John (1608–1674 C.E.). Born in London and received an elite education with help from his wealthy father. Milton enrolled at Christ's College, Cambridge, where he received his M.A. but continued his learning far beyond his university education. He traveled extensively before returning to England, where he began to write tracts supporting the Puritan and Parliamentary factions of the English Civil War and played various roles in the Commonwealth government of Oliver Cromwell. After Cromwell's death and the restoration of the monarchy, Milton went into hiding, was arrested, and was briefly imprisoned. Upon his release, he lived quietly in London for the remainder of his life, gradually going blind. At this late stage in his life, Milton published *Paradise Lost*, an epic poem recounting the Fall of Adam and Eve.

Nietzsche, Friedrich (1844–1900 C.E.). Born and raised in Röcken, a small town near Leipzig, the son of a Lutheran minister who died when he was 5. Nietzsche enrolled at the University of Bonn to study theology but turned to philology after losing his faith. He was considered the most brilliant and promising of scholars and became professor at the University of Basel at age 24—still a near-record in classical studies. He served as a medical orderly in the Franco-Prussian War, confronting the horrors of that conflict and suffering a series of ailments as a result. Nietzsche returned to Switzerland, where he became increasingly disillusioned with German culture and academia. He eventually gave up his position in Basel and lived the life of a wandering writer. His writing became increasingly provocative, and he continued to write prolifically until a mental collapse in January 1889, when he was 44. His many books were all written between 1872 and 1889, and most of them in his last few years of sanity.

Plato (428–347 B.C.E.). Born in Athens, the son of Ariston, a prominent aristocrat. As a young man, Plato seems to have traveled extensively before returning to Athens, with ambitions to be a poet; there, he became a disciple of Socrates. He wrote philosophical dialogues, almost all of which feature Socrates as the main character, and eventually founded his own school, the Academy, where he later became the teacher of Aristotle, among others. Alfred North Whitehead once said that all of philosophy is but a series of footnotes to Plato.

Bibliography

Adams, Marilyn McCord, and Robert Merrihew Adams, eds. *The Problem of Evil*. Oxford Readings in Philosophy Series. New York: Oxford University Press, 1990.

Anderson, Gary. *The Genesis of Perfection: Adam and Eve in Jewish and Christian Imagination*. Louisville, KY: Westminster/John Knox, 2001. A vivid study of how Jews and Christians understood the story of Adam and Eve in the four or five centuries after Jesus.

———. *Sin: A History*. New Haven: Yale University Press, 2009. Just what the title says: a history of Christian (and some Jewish) thought about sin.

Anselm. *Anselm of Canterbury: The Major Works*. Edited by Brian Davies and G. R. Evans. New York: Oxford University Press, 1998. A great collection of Anselm's philosophical and theological treatises. "On the Fall of the Devil" is here, in about as clear a translation as one can hope for, which doesn't mean it is easy reading.

Antognazza, M. R. *Leibniz: An Intellectual Biography*. New York: Cambridge University Press, 2008.

Aquinas, Thomas. *On Evil*. Edited by Brian Davies. Translated by Richard Regan. New York: Oxford University Press, 2003.

———. *Summa Theologiae*. Translated by the Fathers of the American Dominican Province. Notre Dame, IN: Christian Classics, 1981.

Arendt, Hannah. *The Origins of Totalitarianism*. Rev. ed. New York: Harcourt Brace Jovanovich, 1968 (1951).

Aristotle. *Nichomachean Ethics*. Translated by Terence Irwin. Indianapolis: Hackett, 1985.

————. *Poetics*. Translated by Richard Janko. Indianapolis: Hackett, 1987.

Augustine. *City of God*. Edited and translated by R. W. Dyson. New York: Cambridge University Press, 1998. A magisterial retranslation of the whole of this massive book, this translation of the *City of God* should last English-speaking readers for another 50 years or so.

————. *Confessions*. Translated by Maria Boulding, O.S.B. Hyde Park, NY: New City Press, 1997. There are many translations of the *Confessions*, and many of them are good for different reasons (who can resist a translation by someone named Pine-Coffin?), but this is perhaps the clearest.

Awn, Peter J. *Satan's Tragedy and Redemption: Iblis in Sufi Psychology*. Leiden: E.J. Brill, 1983.

Barth, Karl. *Karl Barth: Theologian of Freedom*. Edited by Clifford Green. Minneapolis: Fortress Press, 1991.

Beer, Anna. *Milton: Poet, Pamphleteer, and Patriot*. London: Bloomsbury, 2008.

Bouchard, Larry D. *Tragic Method and Tragic Theology*. University Park, PA: Pennsylvania State University Press, 1989.

Bowker, John. *Problems of Suffering in Religions of the World*. Cambridge: Cambridge University Press, 1970.

Brown, Peter. *Augustine of Hippo: A Biography*. 2nd ed. Berkeley: University of California Press, 2000. A great biography of Saint Augustine and a remarkably good read; Brown is a legend among scholars and a terrifyingly erudite person. He wrote this work in his 20s but revised it almost 40 years later, adding two new chapters that are well worth reading. Other biographies exist and are worth reading—those of Lancel, O'Donnell, Chadwick—but Brown's is on another plane altogether.

Browning, Christopher. *Ordinary Men: Reserve Police Battalion 101 and the Final Solution in Poland*. New York: Harper Perennial, 1993.

Brueggeman, Walter. *The Prophetic Imagination.* 2nd ed. Minneapolis: Fortress Press, 2001. A clear, brief, but profound study of the nature of prophecy in ancient Israel and up to the time of Jesus.

Calvin, John. *Institutes of the Christian Religion.* Edited by John T. McNeill. Translated by Ford Lewis Battles. Louisville, KY: Westminster/John Knox, 1960. One of the great works of the human mind and one of the truly systematic visions of the Christian faith available. Powerful and searching, perhaps nowhere more searching and ruthless than in the discussion of the absolute sovereignty of God.

Camus, Albert. *The Fall.* Translated by Justin O'Brien. New York: Alfred A. Knopf, 1956.

———. *The Plague.* Translated by Stuart Gilbert. New York: Alfred A. Knopf, 1948.

Connor, James A. *Pascal's Wager: The Man Who Played Dice with God.* San Francisco: HarperOne, 2006. A fine and vivid biography of Pascal, paying attention both to his scientific and mathematical work and his religious thought.

Conrad, Joseph. *Heart of Darkness.* Edited by Paul Armstrong. Norton Critical Editions. New York: W.W. Norton and Co., 2005.

———. *The Secret Agent: A Simple Tale.* New York: Oxford University Press, 2008.

Dalley, Stephanie. *Myths from Mesopotamia: Creation, the Flood, Gilgamesh, and Others.* Oxford World's Classics. New York: Oxford University Press, 2009.

Damrosch, David. *The Buried Book: The Loss and Rediscovery of the Great Epic of Gilgamesh.* New York: Henry Holt, 2007. The great story of how the *Gilgamesh* epic was discovered by a self-educated, working-class Englishman.

Dante, Alighieri. *Inferno*. Translated by Robert Hollander and Jean Hollander. New York: Anchor, 2002. The first part of the *Commedia*, this is the section on hell. This translation is good, although there are others. My recommendation is to check out several at your library and see which you think best gets at the Italian.

Dostoevsky, Fyodor. *Crime and Punishment*. Translated by Richard Pevear and Larissa Volkhonsky. New York: Vintage, 1993.

————. *Demons*. Translated by Richard Pevear and Larissa Volkhonsky. New York: Knopf, 1994. There are many translations of Dostoevsky, but this one stands out. Pevear and Volkhonsky are a husband-and-wife team of translators, apparently retranslating all the great works of 19th-century Russian literature in a new and powerfully vibrant (and apparently more accurate) prose. Were there a charity given to supporting artists, I would urge you to donate to it in the hopes that some money would go to Pevear and Volkhonsky. May all the gods smile on them.

Evans, G. R. *Augustine on Evil*. New York: Cambridge University Press, 1990. A classic account of Augustine's thinking on evil. Clear and acute.

Forsyth, Neil. *The Old Enemy: Satan and the Combat Myth*. Princeton: Princeton University Press, 1989. A fantastic work of scholarship that is part detective story, part archaeology: a study of the traces of the ancient Near Eastern combat myth in scriptures, literature, and writing from before the Hebrew Bible through the thought of Saint Augustine. Fascinating and a source for many screenplay ideas for those with eyes to see.

Foster, Benjamin R. *The Epic of Gilgamesh*. Norton Critical Editions. New York: W.W. Norton and Co., 2001. A good translation of *Gilgamesh* that also has a number of useful secondary sources attached.

Frank, Joseph. *Dostoevsky: A Writer in His Time*. Princeton: Princeton University Press, 2009. For those of you who are *really* interested in Dostoevsky, this almost-1,000-page abridgement of Frank's monumental five-volume biography should be enough. For those of you still hungry for more, adjourn to the steppes with some vodka, black bread, butter, and salt and enjoy the five volumes over a long Russian winter. Birch branches and steambath optional.

Freud, Sigmund. *Civilization and Its Discontents*. Translated by James Strachey. New York: W.W. Norton and Co., 2010. Not a perfect translation. Strachey was quite interested in making psychoanalysis into a science; thus, he translated a number of terms into technical jargon when Freud's German was quite colloquial (ego for *ich* ["I"], superego for *uber-ich* ["over-I"], id for *es* ["it"], and so on). But until we have a better one, this is the translation to use.

Friedrich, Hugo. *Montaigne*. Translated by Dawn Eng. Edited by Philippe Desan. Berkeley: University of California Press, 1967. The classic study, biographical and literary, on Montaigne. A great read, too.

Gordon, Bruce. *Calvin*. New Haven: Yale University Press, 2009. A rich and powerful biography of John Calvin, with a wealth of insight about his world, so deceptively unlike ours.

Grene, David, and Richard Lattimore, trans. and eds. *The Complete Greek Tragedies*. 4 vols. Chicago: University of Chicago Press, 1992. Collecting all we have left of Aeschylus, Sophocles, and Euripides, in translations that are both faithful and vivid, this is the foundational resource for reading the tragedies for those without a working knowledge of ancient Greek.

Hawkins, Peter. *Dante: A Brief History*. Cambridge, MA: Wiley-Blackwell, 2006. A nice introduction to Dante; highly recommended.

Hegel, G. W. F. *Phenomenology of Spirit*. Translated by A. V. Miller. New York: Oxford University Press, 1977.

Heschel, Abraham Joshua. *The Prophets*. New York: Harper Perennial Modern Classics, 2001.

Hick, John. *Evil and the God of Love*. Rev. ed. San Francisco: Harper and Row, 1978. An "Irenaean" theodicy, updated for the modern age, Hick's work was fundamental in bringing Irenaeus back into the conversation. Reasonably clearly written.

Hobbes, Thomas. *Leviathan*. Edited by Richard Tuck. New York: Cambridge University Press, 1996. Many editions of *Leviathan* exist, but this is my favorite. Great introduction by Richard Tuck.

————, trans. *The Peloponnesian War*. Edited by David Grene. Chicago: University of Chicago Press, 1989. A wonderful resource for *two* major thinkers: Thucydides and Hobbes. Not just in language but in argument, someone who has read Hobbes's *Leviathan* will see in this translation powerful echoes of the lessons Hobbes tried to teach in his philosophy.

Hume, David. *Dialogues Concerning Natural Religion*. Indianapolis: Hackett, 1998. Hume's classic attack on proofs of the existence of God and of a rational basis for theism. A great read.

Irenaeus. "Against Heresies," in *Ante-Nicene Fathers,* vol. 1, *Apostolic Fathers, Justin Martyr, Irenaeus*. Edited by Alexander Roberts and James Donaldson. Revised by A. Cleveland Coxe. Peabody, MA: Hendrickson Publishers, 1995. The most physically accessible translation of Irenaeus, this is a 19th-century work, but it includes all that remains of Irenaeus's writings in one volume.

Kant, Immanuel. *Religion within the Boundaries of Mere Reason and Other Writings*. Translated by Allen Wood and George di Giovanni. New York: Cambridge University Press, 1999.

Kierkegaard, Søren. *Fear and Trembling*. Edited and translated, with introduction and notes, by Howard V. Hong and Edna H. Hong. Princeton: Princeton University Press, 1983. A powerful discussion of Abraham and Isaac but really about Kierkegaard. Good stuff.

Kovacs, Judith, and Christopher Rowland. *Revelation: The Apocalypse of Jesus Christ.* Cambridge, MA: Wiley-Blackwell, 2004. A fantastic exploration of the meaning and history of the book of Revelation from its composition to today. Readable but also deeply historically researched, this is a tremendously interesting work.

Kramer, Samuel Noah. *The Sumerians: Their History, Culture, and Character*. Chicago: University of Chicago Press, 1971.

Larrimore, Mark. *The Problem of Evil: A Reader*. Cambridge, MA: Blackwell, 2001. A tremendously rich collection of works of all sorts, from antiquity to the 20th century, dealing with the problem of evil. Most excerpts are brief enough to read in a sitting but profound enough to return to again and again.

Lear, Jonathan. *Freud*. New York: Routledge, 2005. Lear is one of the best philosophers working today and a trained psychoanalyst. This is his most mature statement of his philosophical engagement with Freud—yet formulated in a remarkably clear and accessible prose.

Leibniz, G. W. *Theodicy: Essays on the Goodness of God, the Freedom of Man, and the Origin of Evil*. Translated by E. M. Huggard. Chicago: Open Court, 1998. The classic philosophical work on evil by Leibniz. Surprisingly clear reading—just hard thinking.

Levenson, Jon D. *Creation and the Persistence of Evil*. San Francisco: Harper and Row, 1989. A powerful dismantling of Christian presuppositions about the God of Abraham, Isaac, and Jacob by a prickly minded professor. Fun times.

Luther, Martin. *Basic Theological Writings*. Edited by Timothy Lull, William Russell, and Jaroslav Pelikan. Minneapolis: Augsburg Fortress Press, 2005. As good a collection of Luther's work as you could hope for.

Machiavelli, Niccolo. *The Portable Machiavelli*. Edited by Peter Bonadella and Mark Musa. New York: Penguin, 1979. There are many good collections and editions of Machiavelli's works; I suggest this one only because of the breadth of the selections.

Martinich, A. P. *Hobbes: A Biography*. New York: Cambridge University Press, 1999. A great, thick biography. As with Captain Willard's mission in *Apocalypse Now*, read this biography and you'll never want another.

Marx, Karl. *The Marx-Engels Reader*. 2nd ed. Also with writings by Friedrich Engels. Edited by Robert C. Tucker. New York: W.W. Norton and Co., 1978. Contains choice selections from a number of Marx's greatest writings. Perhaps my favorite piece here is a letter he wrote to a friend, given the title "For a Ruthless Criticism of Everything Existing."

Mason, Herbert. *Gilgamesh: A Verse Translation*. London: Penguin, 2003 (1970).

Meyers, Jeffrey. *Joseph Conrad: A Biography*. New York: Scribner, 1991. Several biographies are available of Conrad, but no one has "done" Conrad as Joseph Frank has "done" Dostoevsky (or Leon Edel has done Henry James). Nonetheless, this is perhaps the best "brief" (400 pages!) biography out there. A more remarkable life in its overall shape—yet uneventful in its day-to-day experience—is hard to imagine.

Midgley, Mary. *Wickedness: A Philosophical Essay*. New York: ARK Paperbacks, 1986.

Milgram, Stanley. *Obedience to Authority*. New York: Harper Torchbooks, 1974.

Mills, Nicholaus, and Kira Brunner, eds. *The New Killing Fields: Massacre and the Politics of Invention*. New York: Basic Books, 2002. A powerful collection of journalism and reflections on journalism of the era from the fall of the Berlin Wall in 1989 until September 11, 2001. Focuses on Yugoslavia, Rwanda, and East Timor.

Milosz, Czeslaw. *The Captive Mind*. Translated from Polish by Jane Zielonko. New York: Vintage International, 1981 (1953).

Milton, John. *Paradise Lost*. Edited by Gordon Teskey. Norton Critical Editions. New York: W.W. Norton and Co., 2004. The Norton Critical

Editions are student editions, filled with historical and biographical backgrounds to the text, as well as a number of important critical essays from the text's publication to today. This is an especially wonderful one.

Mitchell, Stephen. *The Book of Job*. New York: Harper, 1992. A modern commentary on Job, which looks like a translation.

Montaigne, Michel de. *The Complete Essays*. Edited and translated by M. A. Screech. New York: Penguin, 1993. A fine edition of the *Essais*, ably edited and translated.

Morgan, Michael L., ed. *A Holocaust Reader: Responses to the Nazi Extermination*. New York: Oxford University Press, 2000. Complementing the Roth and Berenbaum collection (below), an excellent collection of writings from Jewish thinkers and beyond about the Shoah/Holocaust.

Nehamas, Alexander. *Nietzsche: Life as Literature*. Cambridge, MA: Harvard University Press, 1997. An exploration of Nietzsche's philosophy, focusing on his aesthetic view of human life.

Neiman, Susan. *Evil in Modern Thought: An Alternative History of Philosophy*. Princeton: Princeton University Press, 2004. A great history of modern thought from the perspective of the problem of evil. Both gripping reading and profound thinking.

Newsom, Carol. *The Book of Job: A Contest of Moral Imaginations*. New York: Oxford University Press 2003. A vivid discussion of Job, with real attention to the inner logic of the book as a whole.

Niebuhr, Reinhold. *The Children of Light and the Children of Darkness: A Vindication of Democracy and a Critique of Its Traditional Defense*. New York: Charles Scribers' Sons, 1960. A classic and powerful statement of the political implications of Niebuhr's theology.

―――. *The Nature and Destiny of Man*, vol. I, *Human Nature*. Louisville, KY: Westminster/John Knox, 1996. Almost anything of Niebuhr's would be good to read, but this might be the best. A clear and succinct picture of human nature and the character of sin, displayed in its systematic and theological character.

Nietzsche, Friedrich. *Beyond Good and Evil*. Translated by Walter Kaufmann. New York: Vintage, 1989.

———. *On the Genealogy of Morality: A Polemic*. Translated by Maudemarie Clark and Alan J. Swensen. Indianapolis: Hackett, 1998.

Noll, Mark. *America's God: Jonathan Edwards to Abraham Lincoln*. New York: Oxford University Press, 2002. A study of American religion, culminating in the conflagration of the Civil War, and a careful discussion of Abraham Lincoln's attempts to understand that war in theological terms.

Nussbaum, Martha. *The Fragility of Goodness: Moral Luck in Greek Tragedy and Philosophy*. New York: Cambridge University Press, 1986. A powerful description of the way that Plato and Aristotle thought about the tradition of Greek tragedy, one arguing that Aristotle can accommodate the sort of "moral luck" to which the tragedies call our attention, while Plato cannot.

Obermann, Heiko. *Luther: Man between God and the Devil*. Translated by Eileen Walliser-Schwarzbart. New Haven: Yale University Press, 1992. A great biography of Luther by his greatest modern student.

Padel, Ruth. *In and Out of Mind: Greek Images of the Tragic Self*. Princeton: Princeton University Press, 1992.

Pascal, Blaise. *Pensées and Other Writings*. Edited and translated by A. J. Krailsheimer. New York: Penguin, 1995.

Pinkard, Terry. *Hegel: A Biography*. New York: Cambridge University Press, 2001. As befitting a scholar as dense as Hegel, this is a long biography of a relatively uneventful life. But Pinkard—a philosopher as well as a biographer—does a wonderful job of explaining Hegel's work through his life (a very Hegelian thing to do). Worth reading for many reasons.

Plato. *Gorgias, Menexenus, Protagoras*. Edited by Malcolm Schofield. Translated by Tom Griffith. New York: Cambridge University Press, 2009. A clear translation of the *Protagoras* with several other dialogues. A nice collection.

————. *The Republic*. Translated by G. M. A. Grube and C. D. C. Reeve. Indianapolis: Hackett, 1992. For my money, one of the best works of philosophical translation of the past century. Grube's edition, revised by Reeve, is easily accessible yet sacrifices nothing of the depth of the philosophy.

Ricoeur, Paul. *The Symbolism of Evil*. New York: Harper and Row, 1967.

Roth, John K., and Michael Berenbaum. *Holocaust: Religious and Philosophical Implications*. New York: Paragon House, 1989. Along with the Morgan collection (above), an excellent collection of writings from Jewish thinkers and beyond about the Shoah/Holocaust.

Russell, Jeffrey Burton. *The Prince of Darkness: Radical Evil and the Power of Good in History*. Ithaca: Cornell University Press, 1988.

Scheindlin, Raymond. *The Book of Job*. New York: W.W. Norton and Co., 1999. A modern translation and commentary on Job.

Skinner, Quentin. *Machiavelli: A Very Brief Introduction*. New York: Oxford University Press, 2000. Skinner is a tremendous scholar who has revolutionized our thinking on Renaissance philosophy and political thought; this is a lovely gem of a book exploring Machiavelli's life and work.

Thucydides. *The Landmark Thucydides*. Edited by Robert B. Strassler. Translated by Richard Crawley. New York: Free Press, 1998. Modifying a 19th-century translation, this copy of Thucydides's *Peloponnesian War* is especially useful for understanding the context, the geography, and the physical reality of the history. Often used in teaching Thucydides to military officers.

————. *The Peloponnesian War*. Translated by Stephen Lattimore. Indianapolis: Hackett, 1998. For my money, the best translation of Thucydides's Greek; the simple, straightforward prose captures more of the power of the Greek and the ruthlessness of the realities than other more ornate or antique translations.

Tillich, Paul. *Paul Tillich: Theologian of the Boundaries*. Edited by Mark Kline Taylor. Minneapolis: Fortress Press, 1991.

Todd, Olivier. *Camus: A Life*. Translated by Benjamin Irvy. New York: Alfred A. Knopf, 1997.

Twain, Mark. *The Adventures of Huckleberry Finn*. Edited by Tom Cooley. Norton Critical Editions. New York: W.W. Norton and Co., 1998.

Urbach, Ephraim E. *The Sages: The World and Wisdom of the Rabbis of the Talmud*. Translated by Israel Abrahams. Cambridge, MA: Harvard University Press, 1987. A wonderful tour through Rabbinic Judaism, with a substantial discussion of the "evil impulse."

VanDeMark, Brian. *Pandora's Keepers: Nine Men and the Atomic Bomb*. New York: Back Bay Books, 2005. A wonderful study of nine scientists who were most responsible for the atomic bomb and how they dealt with its consequences.

Von Balthasar, Hans Urs. *Dare We Hope That "All Men Be Saved"? with A Short Discourse on Hell*. Translated by David Kipp and Rev. Lothar Krauth. San Francisco: Ignatius Press, 1988.

Weissbort, Daniel, ed. *The Poetry of Survival: Post-War Poets of Central and Eastern Europe*. New York: St. Martin's Press, 1991. Just what it says: a wonderful collection of such poets as Paul Celan, Czeslaw Milosz, and Zbigniew Herbert. A great introduction.

Williams, Bernard. *Shame and Necessity*. 2nd ed. Berkeley: University of California Press, 2008. One of the greatest philosophers of the second half of the 20th century was also one of the last philosophers properly educated in "the classics." Coincidence? Not to hear Williams tell it; this book explores the implications of the worldview expressed by the Greek tragedians and Thucydides in a way that is philosophically demanding, deeply disturbing, and existentially exhilarating. A book whose vision (it was first published in 1993) is still in the process of affecting contemporary philosophy.

Notes

Notes

Notes

Notes

Notes

Notes